KEY IRISH WOMEN WRITERS

Series Editors: Kathryn Laing and Sinéad Mooney

1. Clíona Ó Gallchoir, *Maria Edgeworth*
2. Heather Ingman, *Elizabeth Bowen*
3. Aintzane Legarreta Mentxaka, *Kate O'Brien*
4. Eibhear Walshe, *Jane Wilde*

Kate O'Brien

Kate O'Brien

A.L. Mentxaka

EER
Edward Everett Root, Publishers, Brighton, 2022.

EER
Edward Everett Root, Publishers, Co. Ltd.,
Atlas Chambers, 33 West Street, Brighton, Sussex, BN1 2RE, England.
Full details of our overseas agents in America, Australia, Canada, China, Europe, Japan and elsewhere, and how to order our books are given on our website.
www.eerpublishing.com

edwardeverettroot@yahoo.co.uk

Aintzane Legaretta Mentxaka, *Kate O'Brien*

Key Irish Women Writers series, volume 3.

© Aintzane Legaretta Mentxaka, 2022.

First published in England 2022.

This edition © Edward Everett Root Publishers, 2022.

ISBN: 978-1-913087-34-0 Paperback
ISBN: 978-1-913087-35-7 Hardback
ISBN: 978-1-913087-36-4 ebook

Aintzane Legaretta Mentxaka has asserted her right to be identified as the owner of the copyright of this Work in accordance with the Copyright, Designs and Patents Act 1988 as the owner of this Work.

All rights reserved. No part of this publication may be reproduced, stored in a retrieval system or transmitted in any form or by any means, electronic, mechanical, photocopying, recording or otherwise, without the prior permission of the copyright owner.

Cover and book production by Pageset Limited, High Wycombe, Bucks.

Contents

Acknowledgements xi
Kate O'Brien Timeline xiii
Introduction 1

CHAPTER 1: HISTORY & BIOGRAPHY
Part I: Assembling the Self (1897–1925) 7
Part II: Kate O'Brien, Writer (1926–1974) 23
Part III: Major Works 40

Section One: 1931–1934, Irish bourgeois life
Without My Cloak; *The Ante-Room*. 41

Section Two: 1936–37, to the left
Pray for the Wanderer; *Mary Lavelle*; *Farewell Spain* 43

Section Three: 1940s, historical novels
The Land of Spices; *The Last of Summer*; *That Lady* 45

Section Four: 1950s, lesbian resonances
Teresa of Avila; *The Flower of May*; *As Music and Splendour*. . . .49

Section Five: 1960s, life writing
My Ireland; *Presentation Parlour*. 51

CHAPTER 2: AESTHETICS
Part I: Literary Forms & Genres 53
Part II: Aesthetic Allegiances, Affinities, and Influences. 59

Part III: Literary Strategies. 77

CHAPTER 3: SEXUALITY & AFFECT
Part I: Affective. 87
Part II: Gender 92
Part III: Normative Sexualities. 96
Part IV: Non-Normative Sexualities 101
Part V: Non-Equal and Coercive Sexuality 111
Part VI: Good Sex. 114

CHAPTER 4: POLITICS & ETHICS
Part I: Ethics 119
Part II: Politics. 128
Part III: Activism. 142

AFTERWORD. 153
BIBLIOGRAPHY. 155

The author

AINTZANE LEGARRETA MENTXAKA has published widely in the areas of Irish studies, modernism, visual and performing arts, and popular culture. She is the author of the monographs *The Postcolonial Traveller: Kate O'Brien and the Basques* (2016), and *Kate O'Brien and the Fiction of Identity* (2011). Mentxaka completed her PhD in University College Dublin, was 'Government of Ireland' post-doctoral fellow with the National University of Ireland, and twice fellow with the Irish Research Council. Mentxaka is a lecturer at American College Dublin. She has also worked as a lecturer at University College Dublin, at Saint Patrick's College in Dublin City University, and as educator at the Irish Museum of Modern Art.

Acknowledgments

Permission to quote from manuscript material has been granted by the Estate of Kate O'Brien, the National Library of Ireland, and David Higham Associates, and is gratefully acknowledged. Thanks also to Ken Bergin at the Glucksman Library, University of Limerick, James Harte at the Manuscripts Department, National Library of Ireland, and Georgia Glover at David Higham.

Kate O'Brien—Timeline

1897.	Born in Limerick to a prosperous merchant-class family. Her parents are Tom O'Brien and Kathleen Thornhill, has nine siblings. Grows up in comfort, in Boru House, Limerick.
1900.	Founding of *Inghinidhe na hÉireann*, led by Maud Gonne. Beginning of Irish Literary Theatre.
1901.	Death of Queen Victoria. Edward VII becomes King of Great Britain and Ireland (1901–10).
1903.	Mother dies of cancer. Becomes a boarder in Laurel Hill.
1900s.	Spends her summers in Kilkee, County Clare, on the west coast of Ireland. An avid reader.
1908.	Founding of Irish Women's Franchise League, led by Hanna Sheehy-Skeffington.
1910.	George V becomes monarch of Great Britain and Ireland (1919–36).
1910s.	Her aunt Anne Liddy guides her reading, and she reads beyond her age. Becomes agnostic.
1911.	Founding of Irish Women Workers Union, to be led by Louie Bennett.
1913.	Dublin Lockout.
1914.	Beginning of World War I (1914–18). Founding of Cumann na mBan, to be led by Constance Markievicz.
1916.	Father dies. Family business collapses. Secures a scholarship to attend university.

1916.	Easter Rising. Padraig Pearse, James Connolly, and other leaders of the rebellion are executed in Dublin in May, and Roger Casement is executed in London in August. Arrives in Dublin in August, to complete a degree in English and French at University College, Dublin.
1917.	Sees her first modern play in February, George Bernard Shaw's *Man and Superman*. Russian Revolution in October.
1918.	Women over thirty granted suffrage in the UK and Ireland. The Irish General Election is won by Sinn Féin, with Constance Markievicz as the first woman elected to parliament in the UK and Ireland. First Dáil.
1919.	Irish War of Independence breaks out in January (1919–21).
1919–21.	Regular visits to Fermoy to stay with her aunt Annie Thornhill, who is involved in anti-British activism throughout the War of Independence.
1920.	Graduates from university. Joins her sisters in London. Works as freelance journalist for *The Sphere*. Moves to Manchester to work as assistant translator for the *Manchester Guardian Weekly*.
1920.	Hunger strike of Irish nationalist Terence MacSwiney.
1921.	Truce in Irish War of Independence. Irish General election in August, won by Sinn Féin. The Anglo-Irish Treaty is signed in December, resulting in partition of Ireland and an 'Oath of Allegiance' to the English King.
1921.	Moves to London to teach English and other subjects at St Mary's in Hampstead. Travels to USA as secretary of the Irish nationalist fundraiser team for the 'Bond Drive' scheme.
1922.	Beginning of Irish Civil War (1922–23). Creation of the Irish Free state.
1922.	Moves to Bilbao, Basque Country, in the north of

	Spain, to work as a governess. Begins to write short stories and essays for publication. Her employer is the intellectual and reformer Enrique Areilza.
1923.	End of Irish Civil War, with victory of the pro-Treaty forces.
1923.	Leaves Bilbao. Returns to London. Marries Gustaaf Renier.
1923.	*Coup d'état* of General Primo de Rivera in Spain in September and beginning of dictatorship (1923–25).
1924.	Separates from her husband.
1924.	General Election in Italy, won by National List coalition, led by Benito Mussolini.
1924–26.	Works as secretary and publications editor for The Sunlight League.
1926.	First play, *Distinguished Villa*, is a success.
1927.	Her play *The Bridge* staged in London. Relationship with translator Margaret 'Stephie' Stephens. Moves to Kent.
1929.	Establishment of Irish Censorship of Publications Act.
1930.	Returns to London. Reconnects with artist Mary O'Neill, a former student.
1931.	King Alfonso XIII of Spain is deposed in April, and Spain becomes a Constitutional Republic and a democracy.
1931.	Publication of her first novel, *Without My Cloak*, a success.
1933.	General election in Germany, won by National Socialist party, led by Adolf Hitler. General election in Spain, won by the conservative CEDA coalition party. Hayes Film Code in USA. The Irish National Guard, aka 'The Blueshirts', becomes a fascist organisation.
1934.	Publication of *The Ante-Room*. Travels through Spain.
1934.	Soviet Writers Congress in Russia in August, debating socialist realism. Asturian Commune revolt in Spain in

1936.	October, by communist and anarchist workers. General elections in Spain, won by the left wing Popular Front party. A spontaneous wave of anti-authoritarian collectivisation sweeps throughout Spain. *Coup d'état* in Spain, led by General Franco and other fascist military leaders. Spanish Civil War begins (1936–39). International Brigades set by volunteers to support the Spanish Republic. Degenerate Art Exhibition in Nazi Germany.
1936.	Publication of *Mary Lavelle*. The novel is banned in Ireland.
1937.	General election in Ireland, won by Sinn Féin. De Valera's first stint as Taoiseach (1937–48). New Irish Constitution.
1937.	Publication of *Farewell Spain*. Becomes a reviewer for *The Spectator* (1937–47). Begins to publish short stories.
1938.	Publication of *Pray for the Wanderer*. Divorces her husband.
1939.	End of Spanish Civil War in April, with the victory of the fascist forces, and beginning of Franco's dictatorship. Beginning of World War II in September (1939–45), with Germany's invasion of Poland. Ireland declares itself a neutral state in the war.
1940.	Pre-Blitz Blackout in London. Beginning of Vichy government in France (1940–44).
1940.	Volunteers as air raid warden and firewatcher in London.
1941.	The UK declares war on Germany. Beginning of the Shoah in Nazi Germany (1941–45).
1941.	Publication of *The Land of Spices*. The novel is banned in Ireland. Relationship with scholar and writer Enid Starkie.
1942.	Broadcasting career begins at BBC Radio. Relationship

	with novelist E.M. Delafield. Moves to Devon.
1943.	Publication of *The Last of Summer*. Death of E.M. Delafield. Legal challenge to banning of O'Brien's *The Land of Spices*. Publication of *English Diaries and Journals*. *Mary Lavelle* banned in Spain.
1946.	Publication of *That Lady*. Meets Lorna Reynolds.
1948.	General Election in Ireland, resulting in a coalition government. John A. Costello becomes Taoiseach (1948–51).
1950.	Moves to Roundstone, Connemara, on the west coast of Ireland.
1951.	Publication of *Teresa of Avila*.
1951.	General election in Ireland, won by Sinn Féin. De Valera's second stint as Taoiseach (1951–54).
1950–59.	Copious reviewing, lecturing, broadcasting.
1953.	Publication of *The Flower of May*.
1954–58.	Travels to France, Belgium, Spain, USA, and Italy.
1954.	General election in Ireland, resulting in a coalition government. John A. Costello becomes Taoiseach (1954–57)
1957.	General election in Ireland, won by Fianna Fáil. De Valera's third stint as Taoiseach (1957–59).
1957.	Granted visa to Spain. Travels to Spain regularly afterwards.
1958.	Publication of *As Music and Splendour*.
1959.	General election in Ireland, won by Fianna Fáil. Seán Lemass becomes Taoiseach (1959–65). De Valera becomes President of Ireland (1959–73).
1959.	Moves to England.
1961–62.	Six-month stay in Avila, Spain.
1962.	Publication of *My Ireland*. Broadcast of *Kate O'Brien: Self-Portrait* on RTÉ, Irish national broadcaster.
1963.	Publication of *Presentation Parlour*. Moves to Boughton, Kent.

1963–68. Represents Irish writers in COMES, travelling to Russia and Italy.
1963–70. Development of Second Wave of Feminism.
1966. General Election in Ireland, won by Fianna Fáil. Jack Lynch becomes Taoiseach (1966–69).
1967. Begins 'Long Distance' column for *The Irish Times* (1967–71).
1968. Student revolts in France, extend throughout Europe.
1969. Stonewall Riots in New York launch the LGBT/Gay Liberation Movement.
1969–73. Delivers public lectures at universities in the UK, Spain, and Canada.
1969. Launch of the paramilitary Irish Republican Army (1969–97).
1970. Launch of the Irish Women's Liberation Movement.
1971. Feminist Contraceptive Train protest in Ireland.
1972. Bloody Sunday massacre in Derry.
1973. General election in Ireland, won by Fianna Fáil. Liam Cosgrave becomes Taoiseach (1973–77).
1974. Death of Kate O'Brien. All her novels are out of print.
1975. Death of General Franco. Death of de Valera.
1980–82. *The Ante-Room* and *The Last of Summer* reprinted in Dublin.
1984–86. *Mary Lavelle* and *Without My Cloak* reprinted in London.
1987. Publication of the first book-length study on O'Brien, by Lorna Reynolds.

Introduction

As recently as 1988, Kate O'Brien was still "one of the least recognised of Irish women writers" (Donovan, 19). The shift has been so dramatic that today it simply would not be possible to discuss Irish literature without acknowledging O'Brien's work. The communal room of engaged O'Brien readers is increasingly crowded, but critics still write feeling that every essay counts. This is partly, of course, because there is still so much more we can say about O'Brien.

The present book offers the first 360-degree map of Kate O'Brien's work available. It is organised in four sections: History and Biography; Aesthetics; Sexuality and Affect; Politics and Ethics. Chapter One considers her life and career in three parts: 'Assembling the Self', discussing O'Brien's development from childhood to adulthood before her career took off, 'Kate O'Brien, Writer', on her four decades as a professional writer, and 'Major Works', offering summaries and a brief review of salient issues for each of her books. Chapter Two looks at aesthetics in three areas: 'Literary Forms and Genre', 'Aesthetic Allegiances, Affinities, and Influences', and 'Literary Strategies'—including a discussion of modernism. Chapter Three looks at sexuality and affect by covering six areas of interest in her work: the affective, gender, normative sexualities, non-normative sexualities, non-equal and coercive sexualities, and 'good sex'. Chapter Four discusses politics and ethics from three angles: ethics, politics—including nationalist, socialist, queer, and feminist politics—and activism, this last discussing O'Brien's own political interventions.

The rationale of this volume is to offer a comprehensive discussion which will serve the needs of first readers of O'Brien as well as enhance the experience of seasoned readers. Archival research sits side by side with close textual readings, and history and theory work in tandem within an interdisciplinary perspective. The book also employs tools from feminist, post-colonial, queer, and anti-authoritarian analysis.

In order to anchor the discussion, the book opens by placing O'Brien's life and writing in its historical context. This is followed by a focus on aesthetics, mindful of the fact that almost all available criticism of O'Brien centres on content, and there is a prevalent but erroneous perception that her work is not significant in formal terms. Then the book looks at sexuality, which, as critics agree, is a leading concern in O'Brien's novels, particularly when placed against the backdrop of a 1930s, '40s, and '50s period that was not conducive to the expression or debating of sexuality in print. The volume then delineates another area in urgent need of assessment: politics. Readings of O'Brien's work have been driven by feminist criticism, and have focused on the representation of women, with the second most studied area being her clash with the conservatism of de Valera's Ireland. This section addresses those concerns, and expands them.

It is, I think, because of the lack of a general view of her *oeuvre*, that readers and critics have tended to associate O'Brien with a handful of key issues. Once the whole edifice of O'Brien's career-long effort comes into view, and the connections between all the novels can be grasped at once, those nine novels, and the four attendant non-fiction books, can be seen as one long, single, magnificent artwork spanning three decades.

......

The critical assessment of O'Brien's work has seen a resurgence in the new century, building on the small but important body of criticism before it. The following is a brief review of salient work. In terms of biographical and autobiographical intersections with O'Brien's writing, there are a number of useful sources. O'Brien wrote a sustained piece of autobiography, the television documentary *Kate O'Brien: Self-Portrait*, her one and only "attempt at some decent straight-forward representational drawing" of herself (RTÉ, 1962), although she also included autobiographical material in *My Ireland* (1962) and *Presentation Parlour* (2001). There are several biographical portraits of Kate O'Brien: Lorna Reynolds gave an account of O'Brien's life up to her marriage in *Kate O'Brien, A Literary Portrait* in 1987, Eibhear Walshe published the long-awaited first full biography, *Kate O'Brien, A Writing Life*, in 2006, several friends and acquaintances have shared their recollections of O'Brien at the annual 'Kate O'Brien Weekend' in Limerick since 1984 —with some papers collected in *With Warmest Love*, edited by John Logan in 1994, and *Faithful Companions*, edited by Mary Coll in 2009—and I discussed her Basque sojourn in *Kate O'Brien and the Fiction of Identity* in 2011. All these texts inform Chapter One of the present volume.

The representation of women in Kate O'Brien has been discussed widely, including Margaret Lawrence as early as 1936 in her book *We Write as Women (The School of Femininity)*, which has a section on the novel *The Ante-Room*. Lorna Reynolds' *Kate O'Brien, A Literary Portrait* (1987) considered O'Brien's female characters in terms of their historical significance, Adele Dalsimer offered a comprehensive analysis of those characters in *Kate O'Brien, A Critical Study* (1990), and a number of the essays in the first edited collection on O'Brien, *Ordinary People Dancing*, edited by Eibhear Walshe in 1993, focused on her radical heroines. Criticism discussing the intersection of women with gender and sexuality, with an emphasis on the Irish context, includes essays by Gerardine Meaney (1997; 2004) and Anne Fogarty (1993), with the later pointing out that O'Brien's characters "shape themselves through a quarrel with their social environment", partly because of a "cleft" with "their private longings and desires" (1993: 102). A closer focus on sexuality has informed work by many scholars, including Sharon Tighe-Mooney's monograph *Sexuality and Religion in Kate O'Brien's Fiction* (2008), and essays on lesbian representation by Emma Donoghue (1993; 1995; 2019) and Tina O'Toole (2000), heterosexual representation by Patricia Coughlan (1993; 1994), and non-normative representation by A.L. Mentxaka (2011; 2015) and Anne Fogarty (1993; 2017).

The Irish context has been considered by many critics in relation to an array of topics, most recently in a special issue on Kate O'Brien edited by Paige Reynolds for the *Irish University Review*, in 2020. Earlier work has discussed O'Brien's once marginal place in the Irish literary canon, with commentators such as Eibhear Walshe (1993; 2018), Katie Donovan (1988), Anne Owens Weekes (1990), or a number of contributors in the special issue on Kate O'Brien edited by John Jordan for *The Stony Thursday Book* journal in 1981. Her engagement with de Valera's Ireland as a challenging voice has been addressed among others by Anna Tekkell (2018), Tony Roche (2020), and Fintan O'Toole (2001; 2016). The relevance and ambivalence of religion in O'Brien's work has been analysed among others by Sharon Tighe-Mooney (2008; 2009; 2011), Eamon Maher (1999; 2007; 2011), John Logan (1992), and Elizabeth Cullingford (2007). Class issues have been discussed by, among others, Declan Kiberd (2000), Yolanda González Molano (2004), Caitriona Clear (2009), and Charlie Travis (2009), and many agree with Travis that O'Brien did not simply describe "the social and political milieu of the Catholic petite bourgeoisie" in Ireland, but she "dissected and critiqued" it (2009: 323). O'Brien's work was banned in Ireland, and the issue of censorship has attracted considerable attention, by scholars such as Jana Fishcherova (2018), Marisol Morales Ladrón (2010), and Brad Kent (2010). O'Brien's political beliefs and attitudes have been discussed by scholars such as A.L. Mentxaka (2011),

INTRODUCTION

Anne Fogarty (1999), and Michael G. Cronin (2010).

O'Brien's links to Spain and the Basque Country have been discussed by Jane Davison in her monograph *Kate O'Brien and Spanish Literary Culture* (2017), by A.L. Mentxaka in the monographs *Kate O'Brien and the Fiction of Identity* (2011), and *The Postcolonial Traveller: Kate O'Brien and the Basques* (2016), and by Utte Anna Mittermaier within a wider context in *Images of Spain in Irish Literature, 1922–1975* (2017). O'Brien's plays and interest in drama have been discussed by several scholars including Tony Roche (1993, 2018) and James Moran (2018), her modernism among others by A.L. Mentxaka (2011, 2018), Anne Fogarty (2014), Gerardine Meaney (2019), and Paige Reynolds (2009; 2018), the influence of the 'Generation of 98' by Jane Davison (2017) and A.L. Mentxaka (2011, 2016), and O'Brien's relationship with the New Woman movement by Tina O'Toole (2013). Her approach to the self and memoir have been analysed by Margaret O'Neill (2018), A.L. Mentxaka (2011), and Anne Jamison (2012), and psychoanalytically-inflected readings have been provided among others by Anne Fogarty (1993; 2017), Gerardine Meaney (1997), Heather Ingman (2013), and Joseph Valente with Margot Backus (2013). Travel and a sense of place in O'Brien have been discussed by Charles Travis (2014), Michael Cronin (1993), Eibhear Walshe (2014), Wanda Balzano (2017), and Amy Finlay-Jeffrey (2020). The role of music in her work has been discussed by Fanny Feehan (1993) and Eamon Maher (2016).

Writing in 1994, Eavan Boland said of O'Brien: "She does not belong. She does not seek to belong" (3). In the last twenty-five years, O'Brien scholarship has transformed under our very eyes, extensively and expansively, to meet a changing world. Her work was ahead of the expectations and limitations of her time, and it feels as if today's readers are getting closer to catching up. Kate O'Brien can now belong, and she can belong to us.

CHAPTER ONE:

HISTORY & BIOGRAPHY

PART I: Assembling the Self (1897–1925)

Section One: Assembling childhood

"A writer is someone who throws … herself at the head of the public, and asks to be listened to. We confront you with our conceptions of human life, and our recreations and inventions from life as we see it", O'Brien said in the documentary *Self-Portrait* (RTÉ,1962). There is a link between history, personal history, and writing. Kate O'Brien lived between 1897 and 1972, and her novels are "a chronicle of her time", as her biographer Lorna Reynolds pointed out (1987: 73).

Kate O'Brien was born in the "rivered, wooded, and blue-mountained south" of Ireland (O'Brien, 1962a: 139), in 1897. O'Brien believed she had "assembled … the self" in her childhood (ibid: 36), and her writing is certainly illuminated by her early years. Her recollections sometimes seem tailored to match her present self, as in her description of her parents' traits: her mother, Katie Thornhill, was "outgoing, light and generous of spirit, a hostess, and a spender of herself" (O'Brien, 2001: 28), and her father, Tom O'Brien, "was always for gaiety, even in later life against the odds … and … always delighted in beautiful women and in quick wits" with "many friends in England and Ireland…" (ibid: 60 and 70).

early years

As an adult, O'Brien believed that the Thornhill side of her family had no intellectual acumen, but possessed instead "a refining and nervous intelligence of the heart", which translated into a "muffled, innocent romanticism" (O'Brien, 2001: 18). In other words, they were "sentimental", and "curiously", her father's temperament matched them (ibid, 81). Tom O'Brien was also "wealthy and gay", and "a man of the world", and it appears that the Thornhill patriarch simply "notched down [Tom] for his darling [Katty]", and the marriage was arranged by him (ibid, 23, 21). O'Brien had, by her account, "a happy childhood" (RTÉ, *Self-Portrait*, 1962). Her first years were busy and crowded, as she had nine siblings (another died in infancy – see RTÉ, *Self-Portrait*, 1962; O'Brien, 2001: 7; and Walshe, 2006b: 11).

Kate O'Brien's mother died of cancer in 1903, when O'Brien was five years of age. Perhaps she felt as the child Helen Archer in *The Land of Spices*, after the unexpected death of her mother: "She was broken inside; something was wrong which she must have understood only too well would not be put right—and she was content to die" (2000b: 138). Kate's sister May, at fifteen the eldest daughter, ran the household henceforth and "became a surrogate mother" to Kate (Walshe, 2006b: 9). The father hereafter struggled with "long periods of depression" which "baffled" his uncomprehending children (O'Brien, quoted in Ibid: 9). Despite this, she regularly referred to 'gaiety' in her memories of both parents. After his wife's death, Tom O'Brien decided, "very wisely, I think" (RTÉ, *Self-Portrait*, 1962), to place the little Kate in a local boarding school where two of her sisters were already boarders, known as Laurel Hill, run by 'The Society of the Faithful Companions of Jesus', a French order of Catholic nuns (see Logan, 1994, pp. 120–21). "I had a great deal of schooling, as it happens", O'Brien summarized in *Self-Portrait* (RTÉ, 1962), and this convent school was in fact her true home for thirteen years.

class issues

Kate O'Brien was born in "a period of comparative prosperity" in Ireland (Reynolds, 1987: 27; see Logan 1994: 111–12), one which particularly benefited the Thornhill and O'Brien clans, as well as the "well endowed" Cork Sheedys (associated with the Fermoy Thornhills by marriage (O'Brien, 2001: 18)), all representative of a newly-prosperous Catholic bourgeoisie. In her own accounts of her childhood, O'Brien highlighted this class background. For example, she begins the 1962 television documentary *Self-Portrait* with: "We were well-off. Father was a wealthy man. And we were brought up in comfort and prosperity" (RTÉ, 1962), and in *Presentation Parlour* she declares that her mother's family was "proud and wealthy", and her father was "wealthy and gay" (28, 23).

She may have inherited a sense of loss, and a matching sense of entitlement. "All Irish people are not peasants, you know", she explained defensively to an English journalist in 1926 (quoted in Walshe, 2006b: 40). Caitríona Clear has indicated that "social anxiety" is crucial to O'Brien's novels, which offer an "insight into the insecurities of upwardly mobile Irish tradespeople in early twentieth-century Ireland" (2009: 59). Temperamentally, O'Brien had a 'class signature', grating many at times by her superior attitude, with Reynolds pointing that "when she chose, [she] commanded all the aptitude for boredom and hauteur any aristocrat could desire" (1987: 28), and Paul Smith declaring that, to her, "the working classes were [just] people who had less money than you had" (1992: 102).

childhood places:
Boru House, Shannon View, Presentation Parlour, Fermoy, Mespil Road, Kilkee

Kate O'Brien's childhood places, with their gifts and trials, drafted the intellectual and emotional map of her early years. The mention of Boru House, built in the 1870s by the O'Brien grandfather, brought to her a vivid recollection of "an ugly looking … big brick house, with a hideous monkey puzzle tree outside, that was rather near the dusty road" (RTÉ, *Self-Portrait*, 1962). The unfashionable location in Limerick city's Mulgrave Street had been selected for business reasons (see Logan, 1994: 115). O'Brien recalled: "we had ponies, and donkeys, and fun" (RTÉ, *Self-Portrait*, 1962). She did not mention that across the dusty road lay the Limerick District Lunatic Asylum. Caitríona Clear has suggested that, as a child, Kate "was probably teased unmercifully about the location of her house", and looked down on "because her father was 'in trade'—and a trade [i.e. horses] associated with 'travellers'" (2009: 58–59)—a much-maligned community.

As for Shannon View, the "splendid Georgian house, surrounded by beautiful gardens" in the outskirts of Limerick, where her childless uncle and aunt lived, and where Kate felt she "should … have grown up" (O'Brien, 2001: 90); she still ached for it as an old woman, writing in the 1960s. Throughout her childhood, she regularly visited with her siblings, but was generally not welcomed by their 'Auntie Mick', who was particularly "mean and cruel to children" (ibid, 92). Shannon View undoubtedly inspired River Hill (see Logan, 1994: 118), the imposing mansion on the bank of the Shannon river owned by the Considines (modelled on the O'Briens) in her first novel, in an imaginative 'reappropriation' of the house.

The Convent of the Presentation, where two of her aunts lived as cloistered nuns, was to inspire her group biography *Presentation Parlour*. This parlour was, as Fintan O'Toole put it, "Kate O'Brien's first theatre of sensibilities" (6; see O'Brien, 2001: 71). She described it as a "rich and memorable" space, and a source of learning in her childhood (O'Brien, 2001: 57). Those were, she said, "my most open-eyed and receptive years", and in the convent parlour she learned to watch "a kind of long ballet of the smile and the tear, a serialised ballet" enacted by her aunts (ibid: 57, 56).

Regular visits to her mother's relatives in Fermoy in county Cork brought the child Kate in contact with modern technology. Her uncle Willie was "a man of innovations and new ideas" (O'Brien: 2001: 12) who kept pace with progress, be it in the shape of a telephone, electric light, a phonograph, or a photographic lab, to the delight of the children (see ibid, 13). We find an echo of this affinity with technology in the protagonist of *Mary Lavelle*, who can understand "coils and wires" (O'Brien, 155), and assemble and install the first wireless to ever arrive in Altorno, O'Brien's fictionalised Bilbao.

In 1907, Kate and some of her siblings stayed for a few days in her aunt's house in Mespil Road, Dublin, as a base camp to enjoy the World Exhibition in the capital, an annual event showcasing the achievements of nations from around the globe. Despite the wonders gathered at the Exhibition, and the cosmopolitan delights on offer in Dublin—including her first ice, and her first viewing of an ioscope film—O'Brien confessed that, as a ten-year-old, "[w]hat I liked was Mespil Road" (1962a: 111). This road, and her aunt's house in it, would become the setting of her novel *The Flower of May*.

"Kilkee, magical Kilkee" (RTÉ, *Self-Portrait*, 1962), was to O'Brien, for two summer months of every year, simply "Paradise" (O'Brien, 1962a: 36). There she felt "the cold joy" that children feel, a form of "ordinary happiness tak[ing] on an immaculacy, an innocent radiance which lifts it near to what we mean by heavenly delight" (ibid, 41, 34). Kilkee was O'Brien's truest learning ground, her place of freedom, and she associated it with "living alone with sensations and perceptions all new", recalling that "[o]ne lived dangerously by that first seashore", and "assembled there the self and all that it was to be and to lose and miss" (ibid, 36). O'Brien's best account of Kilkee can be found in *The Land of Spices*.

Laurel Hill

Between 1897 and 1916, Kate was a boarder at the Laurel Hill convent school in Limerick city. She received a Catholic education there, "and I was happy", she recalled, "I'd a happy school time. I worked very hard. I was a conscientious and rather industrious child, and I loved my lessons" (RTÉ, *Self-Portrait*, 1962). To Eibhear Walshe, Laurel Hill was "the crucial source for her intellectual and aesthetic formation" (2006b: 12). It was a small institution, with less than forty students (see Logan, 1994: 121), all girls, and as the youngest ever pupil in the school, it appears that Kate got much care and attention. In *The Land of Spices*, O'Brien would later "projec[t]" her child self onto little Anna Murphy, and her current self onto the nun Helen Archer (Reynolds, 1987: 63, 66, and Walshe, 2006b: 16).

Remarkably, "[m]ost of the important adult women in her childhood were nuns", as Walshe has pointed out (2006b: 13), and they offered O'Brien alternative models of communitarian arrangements, women-centred spaces, and professional lives outside traditional roles. Equally remarkably, in the light of O'Brien's continuing interest in religion, she became agnostic as a young girl in Laurel Hill (see Walshe, ibid: 19), an experience echoed in characters such as Anna Murphy, Matt Costello, Clare Halvey, or Fanny Morrow. Perhaps in tune with her questioning spirit, as a child Kate was "an omnivorous reader. Anything from the Bible down to the three-penny Diamond Library, boy-school stories, anything would do me" (RTÉ, *Self-Portrait*, 1962). Inspired by one of her teachers, after 1910 Kate became a *gaeilgeoir*, an Irish speaker and language enthusiast, an interest that waned in 1916, with her disappointment at the language teaching methods she encountered in college.

assault

While O'Brien insisted that "we had a bourgeoise, and sheltered, and happy childhood" (RTÉ, *Self-Portrait*, 1962), she also highlighted "the unknowingness and the unbalanced young anxiety that were dominant in me" (2001: 56). The uncertainties and upheavals of her early childhood may have shaped this anxiety, but she may also have been victim to a traumatic crime. In one of her visits to Fermoy, the child Kate may have been victim of a sexual assault, as described in the short story "Manna", retelling the assault of five-year-old Josie after she wanders alone into a chemist shop. The story, as Walshe points out, "has the authenticity of a remembered incident" (2006b: 12; see ibid, 11, and O'Brien, 1962a: 31). References to sexual trauma lodged in the "unconscious psyche" are discussed by O'Brien in *Presentation Parlour* (2001: 45; see 16).

Section Two: Revolution
Adolescence and Youth

Kate O'Brien's adolescence and youth happened at a time of revolution, conflict, and new beginnings. World War I on the continent, the anticolonial Rising in Ireland and the subsequent Civil War, provided a backdrop of bloody sacrifice; the Russian revolution signalled a momentous landmark for workers, and a consolidated global industrial capitalism began to evolve into a "bank-encrusted" economic system (O'Brien, 1962a: 19). The professions and the colleges increasingly opened to women. In literature and the arts, modernism seemed to demolish the classical Western tradition. Exceptionally, in Ireland, almost every *avant garde* movement in the visual arts and the applied arts was led by women—Mary Swanzy, Mainie Jellett, Evie Hone, Wilhelmina Geddes, Beatrice Glenavy, (Irish-in-Paris) Eileen Gray, or May Guinness, who would paint a cubist portrait of Kate O'Brien in later life. Interestingly, O'Brien had a small art collection, which included work by cubist painters.

The revolutionary generation in Ireland developed for many a not-to-be-repeated conjunction of nationalist and feminist aims, often informed by socialism, including Hanna Sheehy-Skeffington, "the most consistent feminist voice" in Ireland in this period (Ward, 1989: 246), and an admirer of O'Brien's work. This political ferment brought about an unprecedented visibility and apparent acceptance of lesbians in activist Irish circles which was in itself revolutionary. It included figures such as the medical officer of the 1916 Rebellion Dr Kathleen Lynn and her partner Madeleine ffrench-Mullen, Elizabeth O'Farrell and her partner Sheila Grennan, Republicans Helena Moloney, Margaret Skinnider and her partner Nora O'Keefe, as well as union leaders Louie Bennett and Helen Chenevix and, after her move to Liverpool, the writer and pacifist activist Eva Gore-Booth, co-editor of the magazine *Urania*, a pioneering platform for queer feminist ideas (as discussed by McAuliffe, 2000: 14–15, and Tiernan, 2012: 224–32).

adolescence

Kate O'Brien once referred to "the attentiveness of adolescence" (quoted in Walshe, 2006b: 20). The heart was awakening, and the flesh was too. It was in Kilkee that, "from afar", the fifteen-year- old Kate "[gave] my flapper-heart to Thomas Kettle", the young Irish politician and writer who was to die in World War I, a war that "engaged" her imagination (O'Brien, 1962a: 122). At the same time, she was noticing some "favourite" ladies, "singularly beautiful" women from Limerick who flirted with English officers and paid no heed to O'Brien's "sneaky and precocious watchfulness" (Ibid: 29).

Discussing this period in *Self-Portrait*, she underlined the thrill of getting hold of a "very … passionate" serialised novel by Hall Caine, a then phenomenally popular writer, whose controversial works were regularly censored. Caine's *The Woman Thou Gavest Me*, first serialised in 1912, dealt with domestic abuse, adultery, and illegitimacy, against the backdrop of a Catholic conscience. It "horrified and startled" the adolescent Kate, but it ultimately "delighted" her (RTÉ, *Self-Portrait*, 1962), a fraught first taste of literary romance. Her novel *The Land of Spices* describes waves of passionate same-sex crushes among classmates (*Schwärmerei*). In the all-girl Laurel Hill, the lesbosocial context would have offered opportunities for the kind of lesbian aesthetic awakening O'Brien describes via the autobiographical Anna in *The Land of Spices*, who suddenly sees her pretty classmate Pilar "in a new way", and although "[s]he did not understand this translation of the ordinary, she could only accept it and wait; but her heart leapt premonitorily" (2000b: 271).

As the girl Kate grew up, her cultural world stretched in various directions. Her immediate family enjoyed singing at home and "loved the theatre" (O'Brien, 2001: 36; see 72). In Fermoy, she went to "'the pictures', as we said in 1912", when Kate's "chief craze" was actor Pearl White (Ibid: 37). Crucially, her 'Auntie Mick', Anne Liddy, the "grudging and cold" chatelaine of Shannon View (ibid: 93), became against the odds a key mentor. Anne "bought and understood books", and showed Kate "how to read, and made me read beyond my age" (ibid, 91, 92). She introduced O'Brien to George Eliot, the Brontës, Macaulay, Pope, Milton, and Byron, "told me about their lives, and their ... places in history and literature ... and examined me on them closely" (ibid: 92). O'Brien admitted that "I owe her much of what I might prefer to call my self-education" (ibid: 93).

youth

1916 proved a crucial year for the young Kate. Her father died, the family business collapsed, and the children found themselves without financial support. She somehow secured funds to study English and French at the Catholic University of Ireland, later called University College Dublin (see Reynolds, 1987: 33, and Walshe, 2006b: 21), and arrived in the capital four months after the Easter Rising. It was a "theatre of tragedy" (O'Brien, 1962a: 112), but she remained in the wings: "we lived with the unappeasable and the unmerciful, among flames that we did not see and oaths and curses that we did not hear" (ibid, 114). Later realising her "blinkers", at the time O'Brien did not support the Rising, unable to "understand what Ireland was about—or, in so far as I did, I questioned it" (Ibid, 114, 112). This was true of most Irish people before the British crown executed the leaders of the rebellion, which outraged the public. But in 1916, O'Brien was already, as she put it, "a green non-fanatic and, it must be said, non-patriot" (ibid, 113). Her political self-education included anti-colonial nationalist friends whom she respected, having "communism explained to me, by the golden-haired, contemptuous and impatient David Sears" (O'Brien, 1955: 7), and consorting with "poets and anarchists" (O'Brien, 1962a: 116).

Her life in college, after she "became almost overnight extremely lazy, a lazy and sceptical student" (RTÉ, *Self-Portrait*, 1962), was a life "of the detached and self-centred kind that students live" (O'Brien, 1962a: 111). She was "half-starved" at the nun-run Loreto Hall Girls Residence, and "frozen and damp and for the most part under-washed, I'd say", but O'Brien and her student friends were "delighted with ourselves and our wit" (ibid, 113). Her friend Violet Connolly introduced her to the extraordinary just-published poems of Manley Hopkins (O'Brien, 1955: 7), and many students read Joyce—former graduate of UCD—"with amazement" (O'Brien, 1962a: 117). To her, the best thing about those years was "the friends I made … a brilliant lot of people … [who] were a revelation to me, and a liberal education" (RTÉ, *Self-Portrait*, 1962). But two lecturers did make an impression: her English tutor the poet Austin Clarke, who found "the outward sign of inward grace" in her essays, and her lecturer in French poetry Roger Chauviré, listening to whom, she said, "[I] grew up" (paraphrased by Reynolds, 1987: 35).

Dublin also had other attractions, from the "marvellous" Reading Room at the National Library (quoted in Reynolds, 1987: 34), to the undiluted "excellence" of the acting at the Abbey, where she got a "good all-round schooling in the art of the theatre" (O'Brien, 1962a: 118). Her first outing to the theatre in Dublin was to see Shaw's *Man and Superman* in February 2017, which literally electrified her: "I came out afraid to breathe; I felt as if I had been filled within by some very brittle, burning kind of light. I was astonished"; lines rang in her mind for days "like icicles clashing" (ibid: 117). Crucially, she was shocked at "the realisation that one did not have to agree with one word said" (ibid)—an insight which must have unclenched O'Brien's thinking, given that in 1939 it is repeated by the "non-doctrinaire" novelist Matt in *Pray for the Wanderer* (1951:119), and in 1962 she underlined it when describing "our strange profession" (RTÉ, *Self-Portrait*, 1962).

1920s: War of Independence

The Irish War of Independence and the Easter Rising had been preceded by a "quiet revolution", as Roy Foster called it, "in the hearts and minds of young middle-class Irish people from the 1890s onwards", a generation that brought about change "through the construction of a shared culture" critical of the *status quo* (331, 8). Some of Kate O'Brien's educators and role models belonged to this group. In her holidays from college, O'Brien stayed in Fermoy, and experienced the War of Independence through her aunt, Annie Thornhill, who engaged in her own form of resistance by refusing to serve the "brutal" 'Black and Tans' in her shop, giving exhausting night-long 'curfew parties', and hiding rebels (O'Brien, 2001: 111, see 112 and 116). Like the protagonist of *Mary Lavelle*, Kate probably assisted in some illegal activities. Around the same time, a chapter closed with the blow of the death of Kate's beloved brother and friend Tom, and the sale of Boru House, in 1918. The Irish General Election that year gave majority to the pro-Independence Sinn Fein, resulting in the illegal First Dáil, with Éamon de Valera as Taoiseach, and the socialist feminist Constance Markievicz (co-founder in 1909 of the militaristic Fianna Éireann) as Minister for Labour. O'Brien did not leave any commentary on this crucial historical development.

1920s: Manchester, London, Washington

Kate O'Brien's graduation in 1920 launched her wage-earning and her travels—in the next two years, she worked in Manchester, London, and Washington. Job-hunting in London was a familiar undertaking for Irish graduates; two sisters already lived there, and O'Brien found work as freelance journalist for *The Sphere*. In the autumn of 1920, she secured a well-paid job in Manchester as assistant translator on the Foreign Language Department of *The Manchester Guardian Weekly* (see Reynolds, 1987: 36). She remembered her weekends in London, with "riches" to spend (*Self-Portrait*), the beginning of a life-long habit of spending money "like wildfire" (Reynolds, 1987: 38). She lodged on various Manchester boarding houses, later informing her first play (see Walshe, 2006b: 25–6). As an Irish Catholic in England, she met with some hostility. During the dramatic hunger strike of Terence MacSwiney in London's Brixton Jail, a colleague at the paper taunted her daily—"Sixty one days fasting, and you still think he's fasting, Miss O'Brien?"—and she never forgot his cruelty (RTÉ, *Self-Portrait*, 1962).

In 1921, the *Manchester Guardian Weekly* folded their Foreign section, and O'Brien returned to London to work as a teacher of English, French, and History at the Institute of the Blessed Virgin Mary in Hampstead, a Catholic girls school run by Ursuline nuns (see Walshe, 2006b: 26). Lacking experience and commitment, it appears that she was lax and disorganised as a teacher (see ibid: 26–7). However, she was a success with the students, a number of whom developed a romantic "cult" around her, including a girl named Mary O'Neill, whose mother was prompted to call to the school alarmed by the commotion, only to be told by the Reverend Mother: "The truth is that the beloved is very beautiful" (quoted in Ibid: 27). O'Brien and the student corresponded after the course ended —Kate was 23 and Mary 13—and the pair's lives would become entwined a few years later. At this time, O'Brien also met the Dutch Gustaaf Renier, then a freelance journalist and translator like herself, a former Catholic seminarian, who according to Eibhear Walshe was "either homosexual or bisexual" (2006b: 33; see ibid: 32). Renier "wanted to marry her" (Reynolds, *Portrait* 36), but was rebuked by O'Brien. In *Distinguished Villa*, the autobiographical Frances is persistently pursued by the "tall and gay and conventional" Alec (O'Brien, 1926: 18–9, 22), a version of Gustaaf.

In August 1921, just after a truce had been agreed in the Irish War of Independence, the Second Dáil gave a majority to Sinn Féin in the South, and returned five women deputies, a visible sign of the mass involvement of Irish women in the anti-colonial movement but, as it transpired, also the peak of such institutional visibility during O'Brien's lifetime. Before the year was over, O'Brien had secured a job as "a kind of secretary" (Jordan, "First Lady", 228) for the 'Bond Drive', a scheme to secure funds in the USA for the nascent Irish state. A similar fundraising trip had been led by Éamon de Valera two years previously, accompanied by Harry Boland. The 1921 travelling Irish committee was led by Stephen O'Mara, Kate O'Brien's brother-in-law (her sister Nance was also part of the group), someone O'Brien respected (see *Parlour* 110). Harry Boland, again a 'special envoy' in the committee, struck up a friendship with O'Brien (which Walshe suggests had a romantic side), and the pair travelled to New York City to see shows by the popular comic vaudeville performer Sophie Tucker, known as 'the last of the Red Hot Mamas' (see Walshe, *Kate* 28). O'Brien's mixed reaction to the city would inform the 'New York' section in *Without My Cloak*. O'Mara had recommended Boland to de Valera as USA ambassador (see O'Mara, 1921: n.p.), and now Boland was ready to recommend Kate for the Irish Foreign Ministry, but she told him she was "not keen enough on the new government to wish my hand to become its servant" (letter quoted in Walshe, *Kate* 28).

to Bilbao

1922 marked the beginning of the Irish Free state, legally bound to the UK by a 'dominion' status (until 1949), autonomous except for the six northern counties, a political border which did not match the "mental boundaries" of Irish Ireland, as J.J. Lee has noted (1979: 45). With the signing of the Anglo-Irish Treaty, old comrades took opposite sides and clashed at the end of June in the Irish Civil War, which lasted for almost a year. That summer, Kate O'Brien decided to go away again, taking up a job as a governess in the Basque Country, in the north of Spain, to teach English literature to an adolescent brother and sister from a wealthy family in Portugalete, in the outskirts of Bilbao. "[T]hat lost year", as she later called it (1985b: 216), turned out to be momentous for her as a person and a writer. Her first attempts at creative writing happened here, with a story about the Battle of Roncesvalles in 778 between the Basque and the French, and other short pieces which she submitted for publication without much success (see O'Brien, 1985b: 210; JM Areilza, 1997: 227; Mentxaka, 2016: 61–73).

The rupture of the Irish civil war, despite the victory of pro-Treaty forces, endured for the rest of the century through the two major political forces in the country, the conservative republican Fianna Fáil and the conservative neoliberal Fine Gael, originating respectively in anti and pro-Treaty groups. Terry Eagleton places the work of Kate O'Brien in the context of post-1922 Ireland, when "all the big public issues—the land question, the national question—are now supposed to have been laid to rest, and what we … call 'private' life can come to be highlighted in a way relatively unfamiliar in Irish culture" (2009: 97). In fact, O'Brien's work mixes personal and public, so that, for example, the Irish Mary Lavelle achieves "self-government" when she arrives in the Basque Country (O'Brien, 2000a: 27)—a stateless nation physically 'partitioned' between Spain and France—thus linking personal and political development. In Bilbao in 1922, Kate found an "unexpected Spain" (1985b: 211), one of the most heavily industrialised cities in the world, and a political laboratory: Spanish socialism and Basque nationalism were both born there, and the future communist leader Dolores Ibarruri 'Pasionaria' was writing her first articles a couple of miles away from O'Brien's room. O'Brien would revisit her memories of the "passionately democratic" Biscayan spirit fifteen years later in *Farewell Spain* (1985: 202). O'Brien visited the local Batzoki, the Basque nationalist meeting centre, and was startled to find the Irish flag and a portrait of MacSwiney prominently displayed (see JM Areilza, 1994: 35–6).

Culturally, Bilbao was also effervescent. The public dances in the squares delighted O'Brien, as did the café culture of newspapers and *tertulias*, or debating clubs. The head of her household, Enrique Areilza, was one of the most important Basque intellectuals and social reformers of his time. A renowned surgeon, he was an outspoken Catholic agnostic and anarchist pacifist, and part of the influential 'Generación del 98'. This group of artists and intellectuals focused on the regeneration of Spain after the collapse of its empire, sealed in 1898 by the independence of Cuba (see Oliver, 69), and made an emblem of the Castile region, likely inspired by Dr Areilza's devotion to it (see E. Areilza, "Gredos", 1999). As we will see later, O'Brien absorbed the tenets of this group. According to Josu Montalbán, one of Enrique Areilza's biographers, he became a mentor to the young Kate (see 2008: 161–62).

In her novel *Mary Lavelle*, O'Brien offered a clearly recognisable portrait of Dr Areilza in the character of Don Pablo Areavaga, who has a double, Juanito. It is possible to consider the Mary-Juanito plot in *Mary Lavelle* and the Christina-Denis plot in *Without My Cloak* as disguised autobiography: O'Brien referred to the autobiographical input in Lavelle (see J.M. Areilza, 1994: 38), who reads as a version of Christina. If this is the case, the intertextual detail suggests that, a few months after Kate O'Brien's arrival in the Basque Country, Kate and Enrique may have found themselves, unexpectedly, romantically involved (see Mentxaka, 2011: 225). If this is the case, the fictionalised accounts suggest that the affair had been genuine despite the difference in status. The rendition of Enrique as Don Pablo, or his earlier, recognisable portrait as Vincent Regan in *The Ante-Room*, suggest insurmountable differences between a Victorian man and a modern woman (see Mentxaka, 2011: 226–32).

Although there is no evidence to prove or disprove the fact, Kate O'Brien may have become pregnant at this time as a result of an illicit liaison, and a rumour to that effect was still commonplace in 1978 (see Hayes, 6). If this is the case, O'Brien may have decided to marry Gustaaf Renier to provide legitimacy at some point, and his response may have matched that of Alec in *Distinguished Villa*, who declares that Gwen's baby is not his, despite her protestations: "I can't have a baby unless I'm married, how can I? … I must be married—I must! I'm a respectable girl" (1926: 55). O'Brien's close friend John Jordan, speaking at the annual Kate O'Brien Weekend in 1988, stated that he had personally verified that Kate had had an illegitimate child at a French convent (see L. Callaghan, 2003: n.p.). It was also reported that the child was subsequently adopted by someone close to Kate (see Walshe, 2006b: 36–7, 101). Whatever the case, Reynolds pointed out that O'Brien "always spoke of marriage as an undertaking of desperate gravity" (1987: 36). She married Renier in London in May 1923, coinciding in Ireland with the end of the war.

A year after their marriage, O'Brien and her husband parted amicably (they would divorce in 1938), with O'Brien later referring to their incompatibility as the cause (see Reynolds, 1987: 38; Davison 50). Between 1924–26 she worked as "secretary and publications editor" for The Sunlight League, a newly created association promoting the medical benefits of sunbathing (see Walshe, 2006b: 37 and 42). In Ireland, this was a time of bitter post-revolutionary disappointment. The rapidly consolidating establishment had side-lined "[f]eminism, socialism, secularism and various forms of pluralism" which had flourished among the revolutionary generation and, as Roy Foster put it, it was clear that after 1916, "the secular, anti-sectarian aspects of republicanism had given away to bigotry" (2015: 249, 331).

PART II: Kate O'Brien, Writer (1926–1974)

Section One: Beginnings
beginnings (1926–)

Kate O'Brien began her career as a creative writer in 1926, when her friend the actor Veronica Thurleigh bet her a pound that she would not write a play in one month. The result was *Distinguished Villa*, which was a success, and made O'Brien famous overnight (see Reynolds, 1987: 39, Walshe 2006b: 39–40). The London-based, Dublin-born playwright Sean O'Casey sent her a telegraph saying: "Dublin ventures to congratulate Limerick" (quoted in Reynolds, 1987: 39). O'Brien later described *Distinguished Villa* as "a young overwritten play … over-romantic I think, in verbiage" (RTÉ, *Self-Portrait*, 1962). Interestingly, the first version of the play had to be resubmitted in a "properly cut copy" for professional staging, eliminating some sexually-suggestive material, under the British Licensing Act (O'Brien, quoted in Moran, 12). O'Brien's next play, *The Bridge* (1927), was not a success, and other plays were not produced: *The Silver Roan* (lost), *Set in Platinum* (lost), *Susannah and the Elders* (co-written with Theodora Bosanquet in 1931), *Gloria Gish* (written c. 1931), and *The Schoolroom Window* (1957). Some of these are concerned with career-long preoccupations of O'Brien: bourgeois dramas of conscience, involving pairs of contrasting and duplicated characters including one or two autobiographical young women, in stories setting up introverted morally-bound observers against outgoing and self-serving types, sometimes hinging on an extra-marital affair. O'Brien also attempted without success to become a screenwriter, with scripts such as *A Broken Song* (written c. 1931–2), about an Irish opera singer obsessed with the mother he never knew, and *Mary Magdalen* (written c.

1930s), presenting the eponymous heroine as a modern flapper. O'Brien never completely let go of the theatre. After her novelistic career took off, she was involved in co-writing a number of play adaptations of her novels, but none of these plays made a mark: *Without My Cloak* (in 1936), *The Ante-Room* (in 1936), *The Last of Summer* (in 1944), and *For One Sweet Grape* (from *That Lady*, in 1949).

a lesbian life

If O'Brien's identity as a creative writer became *de facto* in 1926, it appears her lesbian identity had already taken shape in her life. One of the reporters covering her first play portrayed her as donning a "huge Montmartre-crowned hat at a rakish angle and with the longest of cigarette holders in her mouth" (quoted in Walshe, 2006b: 39) which, as Walshe points out, suggests she was "dressing in a code that was recognisably lesbian", later made famous by Radclyffe Hall (ibid). In 1927, O'Brien met the translator Margaret 'Stephie' Stephens who, according to Walshe, "was clearly her first female partner", and O'Brien moved from her Bloomsbury flat to a cottage in Arshurst Bank, Kent, where she lived with Stephens and her daughter Ruth, both of whom were "gradually integrated into Kate's family circle" (ibid: 44). The relationship ended in 1930, although O'Brien kept close ties with Stephie, her daughter, niece, and grandchildren.

O'Brien moved back to London, and reconnected with her former student, now the artist Mary O'Neill, who would be described by later commentators as O'Brien's "life partner" (Walshe, 2006a: 43; see Walshe, 2006b: 48). O'Brien became close friends with O'Neill's mother, the historian Elizabeth O'Neill, and godson to Mary's nephew Austin, again keeping the O'Neills in her circle throughout her life (Austin Hall eventually became O'Brien's literary executor). Around 1940, O'Brien embarked on a relationship with scholar and writer Enid Starkie, again remaining friendly with her after they parted.

Consequently, O'Brien and the novelist E.M. Delafield became a couple, living together in Delafield's home in Devon—together with her daughters and husband, all of whom grew fond of O'Brien—until Delafield's death in 1943 (see Walshe, 2006b: 101). Lorna Reynolds entered O'Brien's life in 1946, and for a number of years the women shared what Reynolds described as "a memorable and stormy relationship" (1987: 83). Reynolds was to publish O'Brien's first biography in 1987, which broached sexuality only obliquely.

In adulthood, O'Brien was committed to developing extended families, and excelled at it. She nurtured a wide circle including friends, family, and current and past partners and their own families. For example, after breaking up with her partner Margaret 'Stephie' Stephens she travelled throughout Spain with Stephie's daughter; O'Brien's ex-husband kept ties to O'Brien's partner Mary O'Neill, who herself became close to Stephie's family, while her own mother became a close friend of O'Brien's, and Mary's nephew would become Kate's godson. Similarly, as Eibhear Walshe has discussed, the children of her one-time partner, the writer EM Delafield, considered her part of the family even after the relationship ended. Walshe has also pointed out that "Kate encouraged her close women friends and her family to form independent relationships", describing this ever-widening circle as a "woman-centred, inclusive web of relationships" (2006b: 49; see 48).

homo/sexuality in society

O'Brien would refer to homosexuality, in 1937, as "that peculiarity" (1985b: 146), deliberately evacuating any moral understanding of it, but her life-long silence about this crucial part of her own identity is a reminder that lesbianism was generally perceived, throughout most of her adult life, as non-existent at best and abominable at worst. It is worth pointing out that sexuality itself was seen to be problematic in O'Brien's culture, because "the Jansenist-inflected

Catholicism practised in Irish convents" was associated with an "exacerbate[d] horror of the flesh" (Cullingford, 2007: 58), and "the [Irish] state's wilful abdication of responsibility for matters of sexuality ... to the Catholic Church" after 1931 (James Smith, 2004: 210) served to enforce this view. However, as the writer Emma Donoghue put it, O'Brien's novels "are never anti-sex" (1993: 183). Discussing the painter El Greco, O'Brien claimed that, although his presumed homosexuality "can be of little use to us in considering his work ... the residue of all emotional experience tends in spirits large enough to be at last of natural and universal value" (1985b: 146).

Section Two: novelist (the 1930s)
success

The novel is the literary form where "she found her *metier*" (Reynolds, 1987: 39). In 1931, O'Brien published her first novel, *Without My Cloak*. It dealt with three generations of a Catholic merchant family in Ireland, focusing on the breaches of bourgeois propriety by individuals who refuse to conform. It was a phenomenal success in terms of sales and critical reception. It was O'Brien's only best-seller, but both *The Ante-Room* and *That Lady* sold extremely well, and *The Land of Spices* was well received. The label 'popular', attached to her work from the beginning of her career, has delayed critical assessment (see Jordan, 2006a: 230). O'Brien once answered the question of why she wrote what she wrote by laconically referring to "Pounds, shillings, and pence" (quoted in Walshe, 2006b: 18). But, as she put it with a characteristic O'Brienism, equating the word 'success' to money and fame is simply the "commonest sense" of the word (O'Brien, 1962a: 122).

an established writer
Soon, Kate O'Brien settled into what Eibhear Walshe has described as "a hugely productive writing life" (2006b: 1). Her

writing habits were somewhat unconventional. She explained that "composition is an exercise of will", and novels "are very laborious, hellish and difficult to write" (RTÉ, *Self-Portrait*). Her first draft was also her last, because she wrote "very very slowly, really, extremely slowly" (ibid), putting so much thinking into each word that when she set it down, it stayed. With a modernist's disregard for traditional plot, she claimed she never knew how a story may end, but her best writing is intricately designed, and a detailed preparation scheme for her unfinished novel *Constancy* has survived (see O'Brien Papers, UL, doc 175). She was primarily concerned with character, however, focusing first on creating a person who was then placed into a situation, reflecting her belief that "novels arise out of reflexions on people" (RTÉ, *Self-Portrait*, 1962). O'Brien worked by night, "a good long spell each night", starting in the evening at 5pm, with a break for dinner three hours later, and then writing through the night, often until 5am (quoted in Walshe, 2006b: 43).

to the left
Kate O'Brien's career as a novelist was launched in the 1930s, a decade that brought about a wave of politicisation that would reshape Western fiction. Her second novel, *The Ante-Room*, was published in 1934. Like *Without my Cloak*, it was a study of the Irish bourgeoisie, but with a more claustrophobic focus on a single Catholic Irish woman, who considers an illicit relationship with the husband of her beloved sister. O'Brien's first two books were followed by two overtly political novels, *Mary Lavelle* (1936), and *Pray for the Wanderer* (1938). In *Mary Lavelle*, an Irish governess gains her independence in a foreign city, and confronts her own values when she falls in love with a political radical. The book was banned in Ireland, and later Spain, which determined the rest of her career. In *Pray for the Wanderer*, a bohemian and banned Irish novelist based in London visits de Valera's Ireland, testing old and new relationships. In this period, two sets of events turned Kate

O'Brien into an outspoken commentator on the left: the fascist coup in Spain, and the rise of Eamon de Valera to power. De Valera's first term as Taoiseach (1937–48) opened with the drafting of a new Constitution including, as O'Brien put it in *Pray for the Wanderer*, "alarming signposts" dictated by the "new Calvinism" of Irish Catholic leaders (1951: 30). The Constitution equated 'woman' and 'mother', and declared that the state should prevent "[women's] neglect of their duties in the home" (article 41.1 and 41.2, reinforced by the 1935 marriage bar). This rhetoric, in the words of historian Margaret Ward, "was almost indistinguishable from Nazi decrees" (240), and such a legal framework ensured that, as Heather Ingman put it, "Irish women were on the margins of their nation's life", for much of the twentieth century (25). In her work, O'Brien pointedly addressed this turn towards conservatism.

This situation was far from unique to Ireland. Women's rights were curtailed throughout the world, homosexuality persecuted, and political dissent suppressed, following a period of relative openness. Art and literature became war sites, targeted with particular zeal by conservative political forces in the 1930s. The Irish Censorship of Publications Act had been established in 1929 (after a 1926 enquiry on Evil Literature), and related public interventions included the Hayes Film Code in the USA and attacks on 'Degenerate Art' in Germany. Democratic elections gave fascists state control in Italy from 1924 and Germany in 1933. Travelling throughout Spain in the summer of 1934, O'Brien witnessed the unrest associated with the 'Asturian commune' revolt which broke out that autumn (see 1985b: 67). The victory of the left in the general election of February 1936 ignited the 'Spanish Revolution', a spontaneous popular wave of collectivisation and cooperativism, engaging up to three million people, described by historian James Woodcock as "the last and largest of the world's major anarchist movements" (1970: 374). In *Mary Lavelle*, published that same year, the protagonist, O'Brien's alter-ego, learns from a Basque-Spanish girl who is "intellectually an anarchist" that: "any political organisation, no matter what, is ... [a]n insult to life" (O'Brien, 2000a: 135). A fascist military rising in July 1937 resulted in civil war and propelled General Franco to leadership. In direct response to these events, Kate O'Brien wrote *Farewell Spain* (1937), to support the left in the Spanish Civil War. Presented as a travelogue of Spain, the book took the pulse of the changing political situation and aligned O'Brien with anti-fascist forces.

Kate O'Brien's ideas and beliefs

"I have always been a-political", Kate O'Brien declared in an interview of 1973 (Jordan, 2006a: 228), and in *My Ireland* she stated she was "conditioned against ideologies and dogmas" (113). Despite disclaimers, perhaps designed to distance herself from specific political parties, O'Brien was attuned to feminism, anarchism, and federalism, and supported left-libertarian radical individuality, as well as socialist redistribution of resources (though not common property—declaring in *Farewell Spain* that "I am not a communist", 123). She abhorred what she termed "hierarchical power" (2000b: 264), and in *Farewell Spain* declared that an anarchist world "would be heaven—heaven on earth", and that communism was "simply the old, old generosity and decency of a few of the world's saints" (1985b: 33, 221). She had an affinity with Christian anarchism of the kind popularised by Tolstoy and, like her character Henry Archer, she liked "indifference to non-essentials" (2000b: 151). In April 1969, in her 'Long Distance' column for the *Irish Times*, she celebrated the end of slums in the once proud Georgian Limerick, equating "self control and ... good manners" to anti-authoritarian principles, and declaring that, "[i]n an ugly world there is still the good anarchy of Ireland" (1981a: 35).

O'Brien was a feminist of the reformist, individualist kind, although her involvement in projects concerned with visibility such as the Femina Prize (she was part of the English selection committee), and her own historical research into undervalued women, show that she supported the collective need for reparative action. As a writer she dedicated her career to the promotion of tolerance and empathy, and made a particular effort to express queer sexualities and affects, proscribed in her day. A "hater of war" (Reynolds, 1987:16), O'Brien was "that funny old-fashioned thing, a pacifist" (1985b: 220). Despite this, she called for armed resistance to the fascists in Spain and opposed Irish neutrality in World War II. She mistrusted nationalist movements, but her favoured form of state organisation, in 1937 (in a discussion on Spain), was "a loosely-linked federa[lism]" of distinct regions, based on "distributive principles" (Ibid: 224). There is no indication that this set of beliefs ever changed.

reviewer
O'Brien's status as a banned author severely damaged her career, but her profile as an articulate, opinionated, left-leaning commentator must have played a role in her becoming a sought-after book reviewer. Reviewing eight novels a month between 1937–47 for *The Spectator* alone, her style as reviewer has been described as "decisive, swift to praise or dismiss, light and witty and always grounding her judgements within her own experience as a writer" (Walshe, 2006b: 69), and we see that decisiveness in her counter-current praise of Beckett and dislike of du Maurier (see respectively M. O'Toole, 132, and Walshe, 2006b: 69). O'Brien's engagement with short-form literature also expanded in this period with the publication of her first short stories. She wrote stories inspired by her travels, such as "Overheard" (1935; see Walshe, 2006b: 62), modernist snippets of urban life, such as "Singapore has fallen" (1942), or compacted memoirs later incorporated into larger texts, such as "Boney Fidey" (written 1956), while many of her stories appear to have autobiographical content, most notably the unpublished "Manna" (w. 1962).

bohemian: 33 Great James Street

O'Brien's social life in this period was associated with the bohemian circle around her flat in 33 Great James Street, described by Walshe as "a sub-Bloomsbury group" (2006b: 54). Novelist Dorothy Sayers was a neighbour, and residents included three remarkable poets and eccentrics: the modernist Anna Wickham, who became infatuated with Kate (see Walshe, 2006b: 92, 54), the flamboyant *litterateur* John Gawsworth and, for a time, his protegé Hugh McDiarmid, communist co-founder of the Scottish Nationalist Party. By 1938, drink appears to have been already a companion (something later corroborated by friends), as suggested when the autobiographical novelist Matt defends his attachment to whiskey: "I'm a genius, my good fellow, and a night-bird! Keep sober in your way, … and let me do the same in mine!" (O'Brien, 1951: 86). In addition to the busy environment at No. 33 and other friends, O'Brien was involved in theatrical circles and attended women's clubs such as the Minerva Club. By 1939, however, O'Brien's financial situation was "desperate" (Walshe, 2006b: 81), and she had to leave No. 33, to become a 'wanderer' again.

Section Three: wartime (the 1940s)
wartime

In the 1940s, O'Brien's novels matched the changes in the European political landscape. She produced three major historical novels taking the pulse of contemporary conflicts, *The Land of Spices* (1941), *The Last of Summer* (1943), and *That Lady* (1946). All three are studies of power, autonomy, and governance. "Power is love, or else it is corruption" (1953: 169), the director of a religious order explains in *The Flower of May*, making visible circuits of power, as O'Brien often did (see for example *Presentation Parlour*, 2001: 40, 43). *The Last of Summer* deals with a French-Irish artist visiting a contradictory Ireland before the break of World War II, lodging in a household where manipulation is coated as concern.

The novel implicitly indicts the Irish neutrality in the war as an expression of authoritarianism. *That Lady* is concerned with a single woman who defies an absolutist sixteenth-century ruler, as she fights for her right to love and live freely. The book offers a model of radical but non-violent civil rights activism.

Kate O'Brien associated her own historical period with an endless war. Writing in 1942, she refers to European history thus: "So far the twentieth century, pre-war, war and post-war periods … And now war again—we assuredly have plenty to record for those who come after" (1943: 45). Based in England throughout World War II, O'Brien volunteered as an air raid warden and a firewatcher in London, as well as working at the British Ministry of Information doing radio broadcasts (but see Walshe, 2006b: 92, 98). The war years were productive in terms of writing, despite the "upheaval and instability" inaugurated by her temporary relocation to the village of North Leigh in Oxfordshire (ibid: 92). It was there that she completed *The Land of Spices*, which was published in 1941. *The Land of Spices* follows the personal development of a nun without a vocation, and of one of her students, a girl who is a budding artist, with a background of Irish cultural nationalism before the 1916 Rising. The novel was again banned in Ireland, which cemented the perception of O'Brien as a 'banned author'. The solid sales elsewhere brought some welcome income and secured a further contract, allowing O'Brien to return to London at the end of 1941, where the following year she began her career as radio broadcaster, becoming a sought-after guest speaker on literature and culture for the BBC, and later for RTÉ. Her radio voice was particularly appealing, Walshe says, on account of a soft brogue made of "English vowels and Irish consonants" (2006b: 98).

censorship

Censorship is a keynote throughout O'Brien's career. In 1926 her first play was subjected to cuts before it was staged in Britain, in 1931 her first novel was privately "purged" of objectionable content before publication (O'Brien, quoted in Jordan, 2006c: 237), and in 1962 in *My Ireland* she was still feeling the pressure to self-edit: "Were it not so tricky nowadays about printing what one has in mind", she laments (1962a: 29). Under the Irish Censorship Act, books could be banned for 'indecency' or 'obscenity' after publication; any individual could denounce a book to the Board, which then ruled on each case, without explaining their ruling. The banning of *The Land of Spices* led in 1943 to a challenge to the Irish Censorship of Publications Act, masterminded by Senator John Keane, who approached O'Brien for support in contesting the stringent and secretive Censorship Board. It was widely believed that *The Land of Spices* had been banned because of a reference to homosexuality, a single sentence, which made it an easier case to argue against the Board. James Heaney has pointed out that the novel was a "very subversive work" on various counts, including its positive treatment of divorce in a Catholic context (2009:64), while its critique of de Valera's government, as Jana Fischerova has noted, was another likely cause for the ban (see 2018: 69). The challenge was unsuccessful, but it established an energising precedent of public dissent and it was a first step towards the creation of an Appeal Board (in 1946). The challenge also sealed O'Brien's profile as "a controversial writer" (Walshe, 2006b: 90).

Spain
At the same time, in Francoist Spain, *Mary Lavelle* was denied permission for publication in 1943, references critical of Nazism were excised from *The Last of Summer*, and in 1946 a note had to be appended to *That Lady* declaring the purely fictional nature of this historical novel which features the Spanish King Philip II. O'Brien had believed that "all my works were long ago totally banned in Spain—and so remain" (O'Brien Papers, UL, doc 166: 4), as she declared in 1972. There was no evidence to support

or disprove any censorship in Spain until 2010, when Marisol Morales Ladrón's research in Spanish archives established it (see Ladrón). O'Brien was repeatedly denied a visa to enter Spain, and it appears she was *persona non grata* for ten years, until, with the mediation of the Irish ambassador, the ban was lifted in 1957. She assumed the ban was due to the dictator's outrage at the unflattering portrait of Philip II in *That Lady* (Jordan, 2006a: 229; see also O'Neill, xii-xiii, and Walshe, 2006b: 75), but her profile as a critic of Spanish fascism, as far back as *Farewell Spain* in 1937, has been given as a more likely reason (see O'Neill, xii-xiii; Reynolds, 1987: 97).

post-war friends in Ireland

With the end of the war, Kate returned to Ireland as a visitor, and developed new friendships with a number of men who were part of a "younger gay literary culture" (Walshe, 2006a: 47), such as the writers Paul Smith and John Jordan, as well as people in the circle of Micheál Mac Liammóir and his partner Hilton Edwards, founders of the Gate Theatre in Dublin, and other theatre people such as actor Sheila Richards (see *Self-Portrait*). In 1946, a formal dinner in O'Brien's honour was organised by the Dublin-based Women Writers' Club, after choosing *That Lady* as their 'Book of the Year'. A cultural and social circle founded by the modernist poet and *salonnière* Blanaid Salkeld, which some have compared to the Bloomsbury Group (see Brady, 2015), the Club included active members such as Rosamond Jacob, Mary Lavin, and Dorothy Macardle, and O'Brien made a lasting connection with one of its members, the academic and poet Lorna Reynolds.

As Walshe has pointed out, by the end of the 1940s, Ireland "lacked any visible or cohesive lesbian social formation" (2006a: 47). In this decade, Irish women themselves receded from public view, and feminist activity looked atomised. Activists who had been unable to prevent the "betrayal" of the 1937 Constitution (see Ward, 203) were demoralised, and an added blow had been

Cumann na mBan's prioritising Republican loyalty, despite having the power, as Margaret Ward has shown, to change the outcome of the referendum that validated the Constitution (see ibid, 244–46). Publishers such as the Yeats sisters and Salkeld continued to respectively promote women artists and writers, but the 1940s represented a "fading away" of Irish feminism (Ward, 245). In O'Brien's professional and private life, however, at the closing of the decade there was much cause for optimism, with the success of *That Lady*, and a host of congenial new friends broadening her social circle. It was in this period that she wrote *English Diaries and Journals* (1943), a (moderately) feminist and queer-friendly book-essay of literary history.

Section Four: The Fort (the 1950s) a bad decade?

There is a general assumption that the fifties were a bad decade for Kate O'Brien, in terms of both her career and her personal life, and she referred to this period as a kind of "Lothus Land" hiatus (quoted in Walshe, 2006b:113), but as biographer Eibhear Walshe pointed out "her productivity … continued unabated" (ibid). Thanks to the excellent sales of *That Lady*, in 1950 O'Brien bought a house in the village of Roundstone, in Connemara, on the west coast of Ireland, hoping it would be a permanent home. O'Brien claimed she always wrote "to please myself" (*Self-Portrait*), but she may have felt freer as a writer in this period, as she published three books with important lesbian content, and tackled an experimental novel again (after what Jordan called "the *débâcle*" of the ban of the daring *Mary Lavelle*; 2006b: 234). Around her, the cold war consolidated a new landscape, generally conservative in outlook. De Valera's second term as Taoiseach (1951–54) strengthened the institutional link between church and state, while the official recognition of Franco's regime by European states meant the embedding of fascism within European borders.

The Fort

O'Brien's life in The Fort, her house by the sea on the edge of the village, was not strictly speaking a solitary life, and Reynolds recalls that O'Brien "delighted in the easy conviviality of the place, and not a day passed but she strolled up to the village to visit post-office and pub, butcher and grocer" (1987: 84). She kept an open-door policy, entertaining friends and visitors regularly and, throughout the summer, incessantly. In addition to many professional appointments throughout Ireland, she journeyed to France and Belgium, returned to Spain (with a visa in 1957, *without* in 1954, as her passport at the University of Limerick Archive shows), travelled to New York to work on the Broadway adaptation of *That Lady*, and used a publisher's advance for an extended stay in Italy researching her next novel. These journeys, undertaken after 1954 while renting out The Fort, may have been prompted by the need to save money, as by this time she was in financial difficulties (see Walshe, 2006b: 125). This period is also associated with heavy drinking, prompting the novelist Antonia White to describe O'Brien as "very gay but obviously not happy" on account of her drinking (quoted in ibid: 124; see P. Smith, 102, and Reynolds, 1987: 89, 93–94).

productivity

O'Brien published three major works in this decade, the biography *Teresa of Avila* (1951), and the novels *The Flower of May* (1952) and *As Music and Splendour* (1958), significantly, three books with lesbian resonance. *Teresa of Avila* is a readable and well-researched commentary on the life of the Catholic saint, addressing her passionate attachments to women in her youth. *The Flower of May* deals with a young Irish woman who, after absorbing continental culture with her soul companion, a Belgian woman, must confront Victorian values stunting women's independence at home. *As Music and Splendour* is the rags-to-riches story of two Irish friends, one heterosexual and one lesbian, who become professional opera singers in the nineteenth century. In this period, O'Brien continued writing reviews, articles, and short stories for Irish and British literary journals and popular magazines. She gave numerous public talks and lectures throughout Ireland, to audiences as varied as the Graduate Society of University College Dublin, the Irish Countrywomen's Association, and the Limerick Italian Society. Her work in broadcasting continued, with regular contributions for the Irish national broadcaster, Radio Éireann (see Walshe, 2006b: 98, 119). Jana Fischerova has pointed out that her criticism increased just as her fiction writing slowed down (2019: n.p.). Despite this busy professional life, O'Brien's financial situation continued to deteriorate and in 1960 she was forced to leave The Fort and decided to return to England. This coincided with the end of de Valera's final term as Taoiseach (1957–59). For fifteen years, novelist and statesman had stood on opposite sides of the definition of socially-relevant art and culture.

In her final novel, *As Music and Splendour*, O'Brien created "a caricature of herself as she grew older" (Reynolds, 1987, 93; see ibid: 94), Signora Vittoria. Lovable, generous, genial, and a little batty, *la signora* is a heavy drinker whose glory days as a respected opera diva are long over. This remarkable self-portrait suggests that O'Brien saw herself as an artist with a past, without a future.

Section Five: 'After' Kate O'Brien (1959–1974) after Kate O'Brien

Writing in 1961, Kate O'Brien described herself as "a *revenant*" (1962a: 38). She felt as if dead, and others corroborated it too. Invited to give the inaugural lecture to the Kilkenny Literary Society in 1960, after an erratic reading she was seen to be drunk, demanding, and rude—to the extent that the writer Frank McEvoy, co-organiser of the event, felt part of "a group attending a wake" (quoted in Walshe, 2006:b 134). In this period, O'Brien did feel that much of her past was "by every good right dead or dead-alive" (1962a: 177), while her present was dominated by "[s]adness, sometimes called reality" (2001: 14). By 1963 she was confessing in a letter to her friend Denis Blackelock that: "I find myself now with little taste at all for life but none for death" (quoted in Walshe, 2006b: 132). As Walshe has noted, "[i]n the last fourteen years of her life … she was poor" (ibid: 2). Penniless and homeless, she depended on the generosity of people in her circle, who provided temporary homes and financial aid. O'Brien's last novel had been published in 1958, and she felt she was out of step with contemporary readers, declaring in a radio interview: "Of course, one goes out of fashion and my kind of book isn't as much liked as it used to be, but that is inevitable" (quoted in Ibid: 133). Having made a will in 1961, in 1970 she sold her literary archive, and must have felt the finality of it. At her death in 1974 all her novels were out of print. Had she lived another decade, she would have seen, thanks to the flourishing of feminist research and publishing in the 1980s, her books on the shelves again and her reputation restored.

travel
But in 1960s, with the loss of The Fort, her home in Connemara, a new chapter was beginning. She took up a nomadic existence again, despite being in her late sixties. Some trips, like a six-month stay in Avila in 1961–2 and some extended stays with family and friends in the UK and Ireland, allowed her to live cheaply. Others were simply a continuation of her previous zeal for travel, which did not cease when, in the winter of 1963, she finally settled for good in the village of Boughton, Kent, in a house bought for her by her sister. She was able to finally secure a small but regular income at seventy years of age, in the shape of an honorary pension for services to the state in the UK, and a new regular column in the *Irish Times* (1967–71). Her sociability continued to sustain her, and she settled into village life, abetted by the "extraordinary kindness" of her neighbours (see Reynolds,

1987: 133), by interesting new friends such as the academics Kate and Jim Hughes, and by "reopened" old friendships, such as that with Antonia White (see Walshe, 2006b: 142). O'Brien's literary reputation still stood high in academic and writers' circles, and she was invited to give public lectures on literature in universities in the UK (Canterbury College of Art, 1969), Spain (Universidad de Valladolid, 1971), and Canada (McGill University Montreal, 1973). She was involved in the international writers' association P.E.N. between 1960 and 1964, while her work as delegate with the European writers' association COMES (Communitá Europea degli Scrittori) between 1962 and 1968 brought her to Leningrad and Moscow in 1963, and twice again to Rome in 1968, to participate in international writers' conferences representing Irish writers.

writing the self, and writing the world

In the last fifteen years of O'Brien's life —although ostensibly working on the novel *Constancy*, which she left unfinished—she focused on non-fiction. She wrote and delivered *Self-Portrait*, her only purely autobiographical text, for Irish television in 1962, and wrote two volumes which many consider to be "outstanding achievements" (O'Toole 2001: 1), *My Ireland* (1962) and *Presentation Parlour* (1963). *My Ireland* is a travelogue of Ireland dictated more by personal feeling than a desire to offer a balanced practical overview, and in that sense similar to her opinionated and energetic *Farewell Spain*. *Presentation Parlour* is a memoir of some members of O'Brien's family, used as an opportunity to revisit her own childhood; it is O'Brien's second foray into biography after the equally reflexive and engaging *Teresa of Avila*. These memoirs have the effect of foregrounding the extraordinary series of self-portraits O'Brien created throughout her career. A very brief survey of these remarkable examples of auto-fiction would include the child Kate O'Brien as Anna Murphy and the adolescent as Nieves Areavaga; Kate O'Brien at twenty as Frances Lewellyn,

Christina Roche, or Mary Lavelle; O'Brien at thirty as Agatha Conlan or Eddy Considine; at forty, as Helen Archer; O'Brien the Catholic dissenter as Martin Devoy; O'Brien the proud Christian European as Father Conroy; Kate O'Brien the established artist as Matt Costello, Angèle Maury, or Thomas Evans; the ageing O'Brien as Signora Vittoria or Eleanor Delahunt. Others follow, "many many more, a long line of mirror images", as the autobiographical Jean explains in *Constancy* (O'Brien Papers, UL, doc 175, 1972a: 18).

If she kept a unique record of her changing self in her work, Kate O'Brien also willed a non-existent world into being. Her efforts meant that the representation of queer sexualities was easier for the next generation. Her challenges to censorship offered a visible platform for dissent. She helped bring about the cosmopolitan Ireland of today, and her wholehearted commitment to Europe as an entity helped develop European identity. Kate O'Brien's pacifism (stated even when calling for armed support for the embattled Spanish Republic of 1937), extended to the "spreading devil" of nuclear warfare, as early as 1962 (O'Brien, 1962a: 32). Her novels of ideas sought not so much to mould minds but to expand them. Her intricately interconnected books helped develop the way of thinking expressed by hypertext and hyperlinks in our time, offering 'jump points' between characters, events, or ideas by way of significant words. As the historical context changes, and readers' priorities evolve, Kate O'Brien's novels go with them, "on the errand of keeping alive" (O'Brien, 2000a: xvi).

PART III: Major Works

Kate O'Brien's major works can be grouped into four periods. In the early 1930s, her first two novels are dramas of conscience set within Irish bourgeois life. The mid-1930s is marked by a shift to the left, and the 1940s shows a stronger interest in historical fiction. In the 1950s she produced work more overtly resonant with lesbian concerns, and the 1960s shows a focus on life writing.

Section One: 1931–1934, Irish bourgeois life
Without My Cloak and *The Ante-Room*

Without My Cloak (1931)
The novel covers three generations in the life of a successful merchant family in a prosperous market town in the midlands of Ireland, Mellick (a fictionalised Limerick). Starting in 1789 with a stolen horse, the Considine clan rises from poverty to respectability in the 1850s. Two people break the rules: the unhappy Caroline, who leaves her husband and elopes to London, where she is supported by her unconventional brother Eddy, and the young heir of the Considines, Denis, who falls in love with a local peasant girl who loves him back, Christina. The family persuades Caroline to return to the fold, and ships Christina away to the USA. The book ends in 1877, with Denis at his coming of age ball, watched by his loving but domineering father Anthony. Having made his mind up to disentangle himself from his family and travel the world, Denis unexpectedly develops a deep bond with a local young woman, who persuades him to stay.

O'Brien's first novel was concerned with individual freedom of action and conscience, a career-long preoccupation, as exercised by young Irish women and men. The novel was a bestseller—her only one—and it received favourable reviews, as well as being awarded the Hawthornden Prize and the James Tait Black Memorial Prize. The novel uses "the story of one family" to represent, in the words of Lorna Reynolds, "the general emergence of the downtrodden and persecuted native people of Ireland in the nineteenth century, out of anonymity into a position of some social success and affluence" (1987: 40). O'Brien's treatment of the topic, Reynolds suggests, is consonant with modern preoccupations, as it shifts "from the historic theme of dispossession to the modern one of alienation" (ibid: 41).

The Ante-Room (1934)

The novel opens in 1880, in the mansion of the upper-middle-class Mulqueen family in Mellick, where the matriarch Teresa is dying of a long-drawn-out incurable disease. She has been looked after by the family physician, Dr Curran, a disappointed intellectual, and by Teresa's daughter Agnes, a stern spinster who is a devout Catholic. Teresa's family gathers to pay their respects, including her son Reggie, an inept and uninteresting man suffering from syphilis, and his somewhat superficial sister Marie-Rose and her self-assured husband Vincent, whose marriage has become a meaningless arrangement. Agnes and Vincent are attracted to each other, but respectability dictates they repress their feelings. Reggie and his mother's nurse agree to a sexless marriage. Dr Curran unexpectedly falls in love with Agnes, but is deterred by the class divide. After some tension-filled days, Agnes and Vincent consider eloping together, but Agnes decides against it out of loyalty for her sister, and Vincent kills himself.

The crux of the story is a Catholic Irish woman trying to decide whether to embark on an illicit affair. Contemporary young readers in Ireland found it relevant to them (Reynolds, 1987: 56), perhaps because of its "unusual" focus on "the spiritual dilemmas posed for conscientious young intellectuals" in the context of "the social effects" of religion (Kiberd, 2000: 559). Agnes is pulled in different directions: Catholic-inflected ethics forbidding sin, a sense of her existential right to experience, and a sisterly bond which is as powerful as sexual needs, affinity, or social demands. Dr Curran and Vincent are constructed as doubles: one's modern secular anguish echoes the other's outmoded melodramatic imagination. *The Ante-Room* was one of four twentieth century Irish novels selected by Declan Kiberd for his canon-forming book *Irish Classics*.

Section Two: 1936–37, to the left
Mary Lavelle, Farewell Spain, Pray for the Wanderer

Mary Lavelle (1936)
The novel, set in 1922, follows the twenty two-year-old Irish Mary Lavelle, inexperienced but eager to engage with life, who takes up a job as a governess in the city of Altorno, in the north of Spain (the city of Bilbao in the Basque Country). She teaches English to three spirited girls, Nieves, Milagros, and Pilar, and is fascinated by their father, the historian Don Pablo Areavaga, an anarchist intellectual who is disenchanted with his marriage to the unresponsive Consuelo. Mary explores this exciting city, and gets to know the gossipy governess colony, befriending two idiosyncratic colleagues: the cheerful Rosie O'Toole, and the aloof Agatha Conlan. She attends a bullfight and feels transformed by the mix of beauty and horror. When she meets her employer's son, the communist lawyer Juanito—married to the trendsetter aristocrat Luisa Carriaga—Mary and Juanito fall in love. At the same time, Rosie falls for a local shopkeeper, and Agatha falls for Mary. Mary abruptly decides to return to Ireland, and before saying goodbye to Juanito, the pair have a distressing sexual rendezvous. Don Pablo discovers the affair and dies of a heart attack.

The novel is set in 1922, just after the declaration of the Irish Free State, and just before the *coup d'état* of Primo de Rivera in Spain. It is a *Bildungsroman*, and a kind of documentary account of the city of Bilbao in 1922 based on O'Brien's experiences there. The novel was banned in Ireland (and later in Spain), at a time when the country, as O'Brien put it, was "newly patrolled by the [Catholic] Church" (1951: 30), and led by the conservative and isolationist nationalism associated with de Valera's political leadership (see Reynolds, 1987: 102, and Donoghue, 1993: 41); already in 1934 O'Brien had warned in *The Spectator* (UK) that de Valera was "leading Ireland away from progress into isolation" (quoted by Zettl, 1993: 43). Lavelle is a personification of the Irish state, testing out the waters of independence. Agatha and Mary are in fact doubles, and self-portraits of O'Brien at different stages of her life.

Farewell Spain (1937)
This non-fiction book, presented as a travelogue, offers a first-person description of various regions of Spain, interwoven with personal recollections, and a commentary on the contemporary political situation during the Spanish Civil War, where after a fascist rising, conservative forces battled the democratically-elected leftist Republic and their supporters. It is one of the most outspoken books written in support of the leftist Spanish Republic, and aptly associating the fascism of leader General Franco to the growing threat posed by Hitler and Mussolini's governments—O'Brien's social analysis chimes with Woolf's *Three Guineas* (see Mentxaka, 2018: 133). Ute Mittermaier sees the political core of *Farewell Spain* as "part of the search for a national identity or auto-image [of Ireland], that is, a consensus on who and what constituted the Irish nation, as well as for a political system best suited to the peculiar 'character' of this nation" (313); thus O'Brien may be said to be engaging in a nation-building exercise. The original publication featured illustrations by Mary O'Neill.

Pray for the Wanderer (1938)
The novel is set in 1937 and it deals with the visit to Ireland of an Irish writer based in London, Matt Costello. He is a famous novelist, but his latest work is a play, *The Heart of Stone*, "a comedy about despair" (O'Brien, 16) which is having a very successful run in London. Matt's work is banned in Ireland, which angers him. Matt is also depressed after breaking up with his lover, the admired actor Louise Lafleur—currently starring in his new play—a happily-married woman reluctant to keep two lovers. In the town of Mellick, Matt's circle of thirty-somethings includes his brother

Will and wife Una, wealthy farmers with a brood of children, Una's sister the historian and teacher Nell, their philandering and intellectual cousin solicitor Tom Mahoney, and the family friend the Franciscan priest Father Malachi. Matt falls in love with the articulate and conservative Nell, a de Valera supporter, who is attracted to him but refuses his offer of marriage, as she had refused Tom's years before, on moral grounds. Matt returns to London.

The novel has been widely identified as a gesture of protest against censorship. The autobiographical protagonist describes de Valera as "a dictator", though "more subtle than most" (1951: 30). Through free-flowing, intense conversations, Matt and his circle—a section of Irish society—analyse issues as diverse as the role of art at a time of political fraction, the joys of finding compatible lovers, the effect of Catholic doctrine on women, the changes under de Valera in Ireland, Christian communism, or Joyce's *Ulysses*. *Pray for the Wanderer* was not a commercial or critical success, but it has lately attracted renewed interest in the context of Irish Studies. It was selected for the project *Modern Ireland in 100 Artworks*, produced around the commemorations of the hundredth anniversary of the 1916 Irish Rebellion, a project listing culturally significant artefacts. Matt and Tom are doubles, two aspects of the same character.

Section Three: 1940s, historical novels
The Land of Spices, The Last of Summer, That Lady

The Land of Spices (1941)
The novel begins in 1904, when the recently appointed English Mother Superior of a French convent school in Mellick, Ireland, Helen Archer, is about to request a transfer back to the continent, as she cannot integrate in her new home and feels dejected, a failure, an exile. At the same time, a six-year-old local girl, Anna Murphy, has recently become a boarder, and the watchful and

quiet child feels lonely and homesick. The nun takes Anna under her wing, and the pair develop a bond that sustains them in the coming years. Irish nationalists pressurize Helen to reshape the cosmopolitan outlook of the school, but she refuses. Helen recalls why she became a nun: the shock of discovering her father Henry in a sexual encounter with a male student, Etienne. During a summer holiday by the sea, Anna is inspired by an English suffragette, Miss Robertson, alarmed at a preying paedophile, Mr Lawson, and distressed when her beloved little brother Charlie is found drowned. As Anna's graduation approaches in 1915, she is transfixed by the beauty of her classmate Pilar, which amounts to a revelation. Against opposition, Helen secures Anna's university education. They part, and Helen is made head of her religious order and called back to Brussels.

The novel is a double *Bildungsroman*, with pre-1916 cultural nationalism in Ireland as background. It was well received by public and critics. It has been described by Desmond Hogan as "one of the most important smaller novels of the twentieth century" (1985: vii). It is considered by O'Brien's biographer Eibhear Walshe to be "O'Brien's most beautifully written novel" (2006b: 84), and by critic Eileen Battersby, writing in 1997, as "one of the finest Irish novels yet written" (n.p.). Critics have particularly praised its portrayal of convent life, and its focus on a women-centred environment. The novel is a reworking of Joyce's *A Portrait of the Artist as a Young Man*. As we have seen, the novel was her second to be banned in Ireland, which prompted a challenge to Irish censorship law in the Irish Senate. It was one of the first O'Brien's novels to be reprinted in the 1980s by Virago in London and Arlen House in Dublin. Helen and Anna are modified self-portraits of O'Brien, and the convent school is based on Laurel Hill convent in Limerick.

The Last of Summer (1943)
The novel is set in Ireland in 1939, as the second world war looms.

A twenty-five-year-old French actress with Irish roots, Angèle, arrives in the village of Drumaninch for an unplanned visit to her relatives the Kernahans, a tightly-bound family who have made their fortune from horse dealing. She spends a few weeks with them under the watchful eye of aunt Hannah, a conservative Irish nationalist opposed to the country's intervention in the war. Angèle finds her young cousins congenial, from Jo, who despite her zest for life has decided to become a nun, to the scholar and womaniser Martin, and the lovely Tom, and she enjoys the company of family friends like Dr O'Byrne and his daughter. Thirty years earlier, aunt Hannah had almost married Angèle's father, but he had become disillusioned with her and had broken off the arrangement, and she had settled with his brother instead. Now, both Martin and Tom fall in love with Angèle, and she returns Tom's feelings. Being cousins, a dispensation by the Catholic bishop is required for a religious wedding, and the bishop withholds it. Irish neutrality in the impending war means cutting off ties with France, and Angèle decides she must return, but Tom is persuaded by the possessive, resentful, and manipulative Hannah to stay and break the engagement. Martin decides to enlist, and he and Angèle leave Ireland on the same mailboat.

The novel is widely considered an indictment of the policy of neutrality adopted by the Irish government in the Second World War. "[W]ell received" (Walshe 2006b: 94) on publication, *The Last of Summer* is not perceived by critics to be one of O'Brien's strongest works, but it has found a readership among those who favour psychological insights into relationships, drawing-room dramas, and off-centre romantic narratives. The bulk of criticism on the novel to date has come from an Irish Studies perspective. In more general terms, Angèle is an artist at a crossroads between comfort and risk—both emotional and material. The novel continues the mixture of conversation and reverie in *Pray for the Wanderer*.

That Lady (1946)
The novel is set in Spain in the sixteenth century, between 1576 and 1592, and it deals with historical characters. The thirty-six-year-old widow Ana de Mendoza, Princess of Eboli, has a guarded friendship with the severe King Philip II. Ana and the courtier Antonio Perez, a married man, become lovers, and she discovers a sensual compatibility she thought impossible. The jealous king demands that she break off the affair, on account of Christian morality. Ana refuses, arguing that her decisions on how to conduct her private life hurt no one. The authoritarian monarch threatens to place her under permanent house arrest. Ana decides to pay the price for her convictions, and live imprisoned. For years, her only contacts with the world are the sympathetic Cardinal Quiroga, her trusted servant Bernardina, and her devoted daughter Anichu. Antonio had been embroiled in a political plot organised by Philip, and unfairly tried and convicted, and now he agitates against the king. Antonio says goodbye to Ana and escapes to France. As a punishment for Antonio's visit, the king confines Ana to two rooms, and blocks her windows. Twenty months later, she dies.

That Lady was successful with public and critics. It was adapted into a Broadway play, *For One Sweet Grape* (the title of the novel in the USA), and as a major Hollywood feature starring Olivia de Havilland, *That Lady* (Dir. Terence Young, 1955). The novel was conceived, O'Brien said, in 1940, during the pre-Blitz Blackout in London (1963a: 6–14). Critics have remarked that the historically-distant setting allowed O'Brien to discuss with greater ease the political situation of her day, including the international community's acceptance of Franco's dictatorship, and the all-pervading conservatism in the post-war years, with King Philip as the personification of autocracy (see for example Reynolds, 1987: 102–103). It is noteworthy that the emphasis on private judgement in the novel is also a time-honoured argument for the de-criminalisation of homosexuality. In addition, Ana's form of pacifist resistance is also reminiscent of Gandhi's civil disobedience campaign against colonial rule in India, inspired by Tolstoyan anarchist ideas and launched a few years before the composition of the novel.

Section Four: 1950s lesbian resonances
Teresa of Avila, The Flower of May, As Music and Splendour

Teresa of Avila (1951)
This is a secularising biography of the sixteenth-century counter-reformation writer and order-founding nun from Spain, who was made a saint by the Catholic church. Excavating Teresa's own references to lesbian liaisons in her youth, O'Brien discreetly suggests that repression of her lesbian tendencies allowed Teresa to redirect her energy towards church reform (see Davison, 2017: 108–46; Mentxaka, 2011: 72–3). The seed of this book can be found on a chapter of *Farewell Spain* devoted to Teresa, where she is described as "the greatest woman in Christian history" (1988: 77). A street in Teresa's birthplace, Gotarrendura in Avila, was named after Kate O'Brien in 2008.

The Flower of May (1953)
The story is set in 1906–07. The protagonist Fanny Morrow is a seventeen-year-old girl from a Dublin merchant family who is studying in Brussels, where she has become friends with Lucille de Mellin, a girl from an aristocratic Flemish family, with whom she shares a questioning mind. The girls are devoted to each other and have vowed never to be separated. When Fanny's sister Lilian marries, Fanny is expected to abandon her studies and stay at home in Dublin, to her despair. Lucille invites Fanny to spend the summer with her, and they travel to Venice with Lucille's brothers and mother. They admire classic art and architecture, and enjoy the local food, and Fanny rebukes the advances of Lucille's brother André-Marie. Fanny's mother Julia Delahunt suddenly becomes seriously ill, and Fanny rushes back with Lucille. André, a dealer

in sports cars, is on business in Ireland, and he offers assistance. To recover, the delicate Julia rests in her family home, Glasalla, a farmhouse on the west coast of Ireland run by her headstrong sister Eleanor. Julia is suffering from a severe shock, after discovering that Lillian and André are lovers, and she dies. Eleanor decides to leave the estate to Fanny, a source of financial independence that will secure the girl's freedom. Fanny decides to begin university studies.

The last novel by O'Brien to be reprinted, *The Flower of May*, was never a success with public or critics, and it remains a misunderstood and underrated book. The central relationship between Fanny and Lucille has inspired considerable debate, and there is no consensus over the nature of their bond: is it a friendship, a lesbian relationship, or a romantic friendship? Tina O'Toole sees the book as a "lesbian fairytale" (2000: 555). The two protagonists can also be read as doubles. O'Brien's preoccupation with contemporary Ireland continues here, in a more muted form (see Tighe-Mooney, 2014: 277–84), as does her interest in European identity. The novel is notable for its experimental features, and for paying homage to the work of Virginia Woolf by borrowing and reworking several characters (see Mentxaka, 2018: 136–38).

As Music and Splendour (1958)
The story is set in the 1880s and 1890s. It follows two Irish girls from humble origins who are seen to have a singing talent and are selected for musical training, Clare Halvey and Rose Lennane. After being educated in Paris, they begin their careers as opera singers in Rome. They become part of a circle of artists and musicians, including a budding composer, Thomas Evans, and a former diva, Signora Vittoria, and they spend their free time enjoying lively outings and engaging in intense conversations. Clare and Rose also pursue their own sentimental and erotic education, embarking in various relationships with fellow singers—Clare with Luisa, Rose

with René and then Antonio. The two friends become respected and famous performers. As their careers flourish, their personal lives meet with disappointments, when Luisa leaves Clare and Rose leaves Antonio. At the same time, their friend Thomas creates a challenging but beautiful modernist piece of music for Clare, which points towards an exciting future ahead.

O'Brien's last novel, *As Music and Splendour* is the first with a lesbian protagonist. Out of print for decades, it was reissued in 2005 and gathered considerable critical attention. The novel has been praised for its accurate and detailed portrayal of the world of opera. It gave O'Brien the opportunity to employ her expertise, as she knew "music and musicians inside out" (Fehan, 1993: 127). Most commentators have focused on the openness of the lesbian content, remarkable for 1958, with Emma Donoghue suggesting this may be "the most exuberant and thought-provoking 1950s lesbian novel" (1993: 55). The character of Clare has been widely identified as a self-portrait. Thomas and Clare are doubles.

Section Five: 1960s life writing
My Ireland, Presentation Parlour

My Ireland (1962)
A travelogue of Ireland, the book offers a collage of O'Brien's views on her country. It reads almost as a memoir, because it focuses on the places associated with O'Brien childhood and youth and is led by personal feeling. The book has not received much critical attention, although critics have pointed in interesting directions of study, such as O'Brien's "eroticisation of the landscape" (Cronin, 1993: 144), or her "unfixed and relational sense of self" (Jamison, 2012: 254).

Presentation Parlour (1963)
A memoir of five of Kate O'Brien's aunts, two of whom lived as cloistered nuns in the Presentation convent in Limerick. The

portraits are filtered through O'Brien's perceptions as a child and a girl, which gives the book a strong autobiographical angle. The humorous and warm close observation makes the subjects feel almost like theatrical characters in a women-only drama. The book has received limited critical attention, mainly in the context of Irish Studies. The critic Fintan O'Toole has described *Presentation Parlour* as "delightful and perceptive" (2001: 4).

CHAPTER 2:

AESTHETICS

PART I: LITERARY FORMS & GENRES

avant garde

According to Kate O'Brien, "the disciplines and tests of a work of art" are: "Vision, imagination, passion, fancy, invention, scholarship, detachment, and the steely restraints and consciously selected embellishments of form and of design" (1943: 7–8). O'Brien has been traditionally perceived as a stylistically conservative author. The vast majority of O'Brien criticism would agree with Eibhear Walshe's assessment that "her novels were deceptively traditional in form but radical in content" (2006b: 2). Many commentators have associated her work with a regressive Victorian-realist mode of narration, and the perception of her writing as formally 'flawed' has been one of the most persistent tropes in O'Brien criticism (see Mentxaka, 2011: 11–14). And yet, Kate O'Brien was a modernist, whose approach to plot structure and narrative point of view, to give two examples, matched that of other modernists. Her aesthetics have unique features too. For example, she is a master of connotation, and her use of subtext and intertextuality is of dizzying complexity. She adopted and modified in unique ways traditional literary strategies such as personification and allegory, and pre-modernist tropes such as the *Doppelgänger*. In her autobiographical output, her remarkable gallery of fictionalised self-portraits is unmatched in English literature.

O'Brien was partial to the term *avant-gardiste*, and the distinction may be more meaningful in defining her practice than related terms such as experimenter, or modernist. She did not reduce the *avant garde* to aesthetics—as is too often done with modernist writing—but saw form and content as allies. In a discussion of 1966, she gave Swift as the supreme example of an *avant-gardiste*, "whose anger and contempt for society were a new assault, but whose prose was also of a new, pristine mint" (O'Brien Papers, UL, Doc 157). This seems to somewhat contradict an earlier endorsement, in 1937, of Walter Pater's aesthetics of "manifest non-utilitarianism" (1985b: 13). Kate O'Brien's aesthetics of connotation and her 'deep realism' were at the service of truthfulness —not formalism, not ideology, not the market. Her work is in fact a good example of "writing to a high standard", which she equated, in an article of 1965, to writing that is "non-parochial and free" (1981b: 37). In this chapter, we make visible Kate O'Brien's aesthetics, by locating her work in literary terms. To begin with, the literary forms and genres favoured by O'Brien should provide us with easy-to-establish coordinates, and we will look at them in turn.

forms

Kate O'Brien engaged with a number of literary forms: novel, theatre, essay, review. Each form makes its own stylistic demands. O'Brien was a valued reviewer, which indicates a mastery of the short form. 'Utilitarian' in intent, a review is no less an opportunity for creativity. Consider the *rhythm* in her famous review of Beckett's *Murphy*:

> It truly is magnificent and a treasure—if you like it. Quite useless, quite idiotic, if you don't. It is a sweeping, bold record of an adventure in the soul; it is erudite, allusive, brilliant, impudent and rude (quoted in M. O'Toole, 1993: 132).

These three sentences are *composed*, with two statements and a conclusion shaped by punctuation: the equanimity of the double iambic is pushed outwards as if by a bold Samson, bringing down a cascade of bricks upon herself, now sided with the "impudent and rude".

O'Brien also had an interest in mixing literary forms. She is known as a novelist, and her fiction is expositive rather than suggestive, but Lorna Reynolds highlighted her use of "the oblique methods of poetry to intimate folds of meaning" (Reynolds, 1987: 47), and John McGahern once described her as "a poet working in prose" (quoted in Kiberd, 574). Her career began in the theatre, which traditionally demands that character be constructed through dialogue. In her fiction, she delighted in dialectal inflections and in loaded conversation. Heteroglossia was of particular interest to her, so for example the protagonist of *The Flower of May* speaks French for the 'bright' half of the book (silently 'translated' by the novel), and Hiberno-English for the 'dark' half, in a conceptual book structure inspired by a lighthouse (see Mentxaka 2011: 133). O'Brien remains enthralled by the three-act play structure in her fiction. Anthony Roche has said of *The Ante-Room* that "the lessons learned as a dramatist … found their way into her writing of prose narrative" (1993: 89), while Paige Reynolds traces "[t]he legacy of the [Celtic] Revival's theatricality" in novels such as *Pray for the Wanderer* (2018: 61). There is often a sense of a deliberate staginess in her work, which becomes more obvious in dialogue-heavy, location-scant books such as *That Lady*.

genres

Genres are primarily associated with themes—that is, with content—but each genre is of course aligned to a specific style, and therefore genre studies is a very useful way of understanding O'Brien's stylistic breadth and priorities. Kate O'Brien is perceived as being genre-bound, with most criticism presenting her as a writer in the romance genre. The *Bildungsroman* or 'novel of development' is in fact the genre she favoured (sometimes intersecting with romance), but she worked in a wide range of others. There is a double bind in her work which correlates to genre formations: a preoccupation with the inner development in individuals, and with the outer action of history. We may say that an 'inner' focus brings together her interest in the *Bildungsroman*, life writing, romance, and the family saga. Conversely, an 'outer' focus is reflected in her engagement with political fiction, documentary, travel writing, and satire. This 'inner' and 'outer' division in fact hinges in the 'thesis novel', a novel where an ethical conundrum (enmeshed into specific cultural and historical circumstances) presents itself to the protagonist. O'Brien's work pays particular attention to this individual-collective hinge.

inner

An 'inner' focus means that writerly resources focus on character building. A literature of self-knowledge and relational psychology, both conflict-driven, is assisted stylistically by point-of-view techniques, subtext, or connotation, as we will see later. In 1946, Vivian Mercier described Kate O'Brien as "perhaps the ablest practitioner of Romance in the English language" (quoted by Hayes, 3), and in 1985 Eavan Boland, with most critics, was still placing O'Brien in "the general category of romantic novelist" (1994: 7), but O'Brien can be equally credited as the writer who expanded romantic convention to the verge of exploding it. Consider the climax of the romantic liaison in *Mary Lavelle*, which continues to discomfit readers. Or the crushing failure of romantic expectations in the family saga *Without My Cloak*, with Christina and Caroline at both ends of disappointment: one forcibly separated from her beloved, the other repulsed after marrying hers.

The *Bildungsroman* tradition was given an upgrade by O'Brien too. She offered a strikingly original take on the genre by giving the portrait of a woman at three points in her life, presented simultaneously, in the Nieves-Mary-Agatha narrative in *Mary*

Lavelle. In *The Land of Spices*, Helen is in her thirties when she finally reaches adulthood—a self-sustaining selfhood—by forgiving the sins of the father; but for James Heaney, this represents a kind of anti-*Bildungsroman*, in that Helen "actually fails to develop from adolescence into adulthood" (2009: 66). The *Künstlerroman*, tracing an artist's coming of age, is modernised, from Anna Murphy (lesbian aesthetics) and Denis Considine (garden design), to Clare/Tom Halvey (interpreter-plus-creator), and Rose Lenanne (learning to sin/sing). Life-writing is another genre O'Brien favoured. Notwithstanding her two biographies and her study of English diaries, she actually made an outstanding contribution to the genre with the fictionalised autobiographical portraiture she produced throughout her career (a series of studies comparable to those by Dürer and Rembrandt in painting).

outer

An 'outer' focus means prioritising clarity and an authoritative voice, with an engaging but unobtrusive, flourish-free, style. As we will see later, O'Brien favoured discreet literary techniques such as allegory and personification. An experienced reviewer, she mastered the 'witness' mode of first-person speakers, stylistic guarantor of immediacy and truthfulness. Her activist fiction is wide-ranging, from feminist, queer, and leftist agendas, to Europeanism, and Irish anti-isolationism. Her contribution to the documentary genre is easier to assess by fictionalised documentaries, such as 1922 Bilbao as industrial metropolis in *Mary Lavelle*, than through a factual discussion such as *My Ireland*.

In her activist writing, she was part of the Western politicisation of literature in the 1930s. Kate O'Brien's *Farewell Spain* in 1937, Virginia Woolf's *Three Guineas* in 1938, and George Orwell's *Homage to Catalonia* in 1938, are three responses to the Spanish Civil War which can be seen to be complementary, from fiction writers who supported the democratic left in the conflict, were sympathetic towards anarchism, and rejected the dictates of socialist realism in their novels. O'Brien's fiction is also attuned to the work of Sylvia Townsend Warner—like Orwell an anti-fascist volunteer in Spain—who dissected authoritarianism and misogyny in *After the Death of Don Juan* (1938) with the same trans-historical robustness as O'Brien in *That Lady*, and who wrote women-centred *Bildungsromane* with a lesbian sensibility.

In Eibhear Walshe's view, with her first novels O'Brien "[brought] an entire genre into being, the Irish bourgeois novel", following on from precursors such as Gerald Griffin and Katherine Cecil Thurston (2006b: 76). O'Brien's 'state of the nation' novels represent as we have seen a unique *historical* record, such as a social portrait of 1941 Ireland's war neutrality in *The Last of Summer*. Her interest in *bona fide* travel writing, indicated by two travelogues and the foreign settings of many of her novels, translates in a keen sense of locatedness as a central element to a scene. Comedy is neglected in accounts of O'Brien, but her parodic and satiric vein resurfaces regularly. A clear example is her "parodic" rewrite of Joyce in *The Land of Spices*, discussed by Ann Owens Weekes (122), while Jane Davison has pointed to the "witty dialogue" and the "irony" in *Without My Cloak* (46, 52). In *Pray for the Wanderer*, Una tells Kate's alter-ego Matt that "every now and then in your books you're great fun… I really think you're at your best when you're being amusing", and Matt clarifies that a writer "mustn't be so dumb as to be merry" (1951: 133, 134). There is 'serious fun' in all O'Brien novels. Consider the pastiche elements in *The Ante-Room*, the teasing non-eroticism of *The Flower of May*, or the Swiftean vocation of *Pray for the Wanderer*. The comic vignettes in the Café Alemán in *Mary Lavelle* can be seen as an invitation to see Agatha Conlan (invariably read as forbidding) as a comic character, a kind of 'lesbian Buster Keaton'.

mixed genres

Kate O'Brien is also markedly interested in mixing genres. For example, *Mary Lavelle* is a mixture of documentary, autobiography, romance, and political novel, while *Farewell Spain* is a mixture of political writing and travelogue. Among her political fiction, we find several 'state of the nation' novels discussing Irish political developments contemporaneous with her writing. In these, the analysis is articulated through an individual, normally someone challenging authority, as for example in *The Last of Summer*. Her political fiction is sometimes activist fiction, as it seeks to bring about change rather than merely registering a situation. For example, she seeks to denounce and contest the limitations imposed on women and the oppression of sexual non-conformists.

As Music and Splendour may be said to be an activist novel seeking to advocate for sexual freedoms for women, through the double *Bildungsroman* of the friends Clare and Rose. Similarly, the biography *Teresa of Avila* may be said to be an activist contribution to lesbian historiography. Anne Fogarty has pointed out that, "by bringing the *Bildungsroman*, a literary genre which is a product of high culture, into contact with women's romance, a form of popular fiction, O'Brien creates an idiosyncratic literary space of her own" (1993: 104). One may also say that O'Brien's trans-generic experiments open up literary space to foster the transmigration of readerships.

PART II: AESTHETIC ALLEGIANCES, AFFINITIES, and INFLUENCES

form and content

This section considers Kate O'Brien's allegiances to four movements in literature: modernism, New Woman writing, the Generación del 98 ('Generation of 98'), and existentialism. Modernism is generally associated with formal experimentation. It could be argued that the other three movements are not bound by aesthetics as much as by thematic interests: respectively women's lives, the regeneration of Spain, and existentialist philosophy. However, no literary movement is *devoid* of stylistic concerns.

Thus, the 'Generation of 98' took the Spanish region of Castile as their model for an ascetic but "robust" prose ['recia' in the original] (E. Areilza, 1999:26). Similarly, for some New Women writers such as George Egerton and Emily Lawless, a focus on female psychology meant a stylistic interest in the reverie. Likewise, for existentialist writers, plot structures had unexpected peaks and no closure.

Kate O'Brien adopted what we may call a 'discreet modernism', which avoids obvious experimentation (for example, with punctuation), and often resonates with nineteenth-century writing. Her work is a bridge between realism and modernism: committed to clarity in the writing, it is also devoted to an aesthetics of connotation. Modernism is generally considered to be a break with nineteenth-century realism, but it can be seen as a furthering of the realist project, by bringing in an interest in psychology. From this point of view, we can say that O'Brien's bridging work makes visible the 'deep realism' of modernism. But O'Brien, like other modernists, also knew that she had to break with the stylistic imperatives of the past. She explained that the theologian and writer "John Henry Newman ... gave generations of us a prose style" (1962b: 6). The stiff, orderly logician's prose associated with Newman was a respected model. For a writer educated at the Catholic University of Ireland (later UCD), that institution's founder Newman was the model to reject (Newman is to O'Brien what Brontë is to Richardson and Bennett is to Woolf). It was a Promethean effort, O'Brien explained in the essay "UCD as I Forget It", quoting Newman's famous 1852 invocation of Ireland, where he imagined a prosperous country a hundred years on. "For one can grow old", she said, "still trying *not* to echo that clarion-writing, throughout a long life in flight from 'I look to a land both old and young...' and the ensuing paragraph—inescapable" (ibid.). Newman's highly rhetorical and stilted style was powerful, which made it all the more important to resist it. O'Brien describes this struggle to break free as "a writer's problem, technical" (ibid). The section below looks at the ways in which she tackled that technical problem.

Section One: allegiances

The modernist movement is both a product and a critique of modernity; it is characterised by stylistic adventurousness, and an interest in the human mind at work. Critics' fascination with the movement has elevated it to the highest position in the literary canon. Kate O'Brien critics have occasionally identified traces of modernism in her work, largely pointing to some of her themes which are associated with the modernist movement, such as the dislocated self, a crushing world, or change as a touchstone. But content and form are inseparable. For example, urban effervescence, another key interest of modernism, plays an important role in *Mary Lavelle*, set in an industrial metropolis, and featuring that staple of modernist grammar, the endlessly coiling list:

> It was nearly eight o'clock. She paid her bill and walked out.
> She did not take the train, however. She turned into the racketing mazes of old Altorno. ... [A]t this hour the town ... was fiercely illumined and shadowed, though plane-trees, archways and shop windows, by torrents of white electric light ... Tram-bells clanged excitedly, motor-horns sounded and policemen blew their whistles; evening papers were yelled on every corner. (187–8)

In this novel, the filthy tidal river becomes a symbol of living, understood as the hurling away of emotional debris:

> By living outwardly for long enough and with determination, all would be restored. A bad dream would vanish. A memory ... would be rubbed away, lost, misshapen by the persistent loading up and tossing about over its face of every kind of rag, bone, and bottle from the rest of life. (202)

There has been practically no attempt at elucidating how O'Brien's stylistic features resonate with modernism. As we will see later in greater detail, O'Brien's favoured point of view, for example, is that of modernist fiction: free indirect speech, or third-person free indirect style. In modernist fashion, she discarded traditional plot, to have her stories hinge around a pivotal moment. Like other modernists, in poetic fashion she paid attention to every word, increasing its load to breaking point by considering sound, length, connotation, and neighbouring text. In addition to her experiments with genre, as we will see, she fearlessly mixed media, introducing cinematic, painterly, or design techniques onto writing, adopting the intermediality brewed by cross-pollinating modernist communities. Like other modernists, she gave varied expression to the thinking self, from stream of consciousness to interior monologue, but shone above many peers in her use of the *Doppelgänger* to embody inner conflict. As we will see, like other modernists, but with unusual zeal and daring, she folded time, not just providing corridors between past and present, but by entertaining quantum simultaneities, by shifting characters on the chess-board of her books, and by questioning the stability of the factual-fictitious divide.

New Woman writing

The New Woman movement in literature sought to give expression to women's interests and preoccupations, including the furthering of women's rights. The role of Irish writers in the movement was, as Tina O'Toole has discussed, "foundational" (2013: 2). New Woman fiction became a publishing sensation, extending beyond anglophone contexts, for example into Spanish literature. Sally Ledger has shown that late nineteenth-century New Woman writing was the laboratory where modernist stylistic and thematic concerns were first developed. "[P]roto-modernist" in stylistic terms (Ledger, 1997: 181), Irish 'New Woman' writers such as George Egerton (Mary Chavelita Dunne) and Emily Lawless also helped develop an early modernist exploration of psychology. As with those forerunners, O'Brien's 'dramas of conscience' are also 'dramas of consciousness'. New Woman writing was also noted for its "sexual candour" (ibid., 95), another important precursor for O'Brien's fiction.

It can be argued that O'Brien is a later example of a New Woman novelist. *The Ante-Room*, for example, could be placed side by side with Hannah Lynch's *An Odd Experiment* (1897), or *Without My Cloak* beside Sarah Grand's *The Beth Book* (1897). Yolanda González Molano has pointed out that "[t]he protagonists of novels such as *Without My Cloak*, *The Flower of May*, or *As Music and Splendour* are, in fact, Victorian characters" (144–5, my translation), while Walshe has described Henry Archer in *The Land of Spices* as "a figure from late Victorian decadent literature" (2006b: 87). This is less a "retreat" (Reynolds, 1987: 90) than a repositioning. The governess-abroad novel *Mary Lavelle* is closer in mood and scope to Charlotte Brontë's *Jane Eyre* (1847) (echoing its plot and feminist yearnings), than it is to Maura Laverty's *No More than Human* (1944), another autobiographical governess novel, dealing with the exact same period and sharing experiences and even locations with Lavelle (the Irish Laverty was a governess in Madrid and Bilbao in 1924; see Mentxaka 2016: 55–60). O'Brien's interest in Victorian and pre-modernist settings and mores, coupled with her unobtrusive style, are worthy of greater attention.

Generación del 98

Kate O'Brien certainly appears to be the last writer of the 'Generación del 98'. A late nineteenth-century literary and artistic movement in Spain, it was retrospectively named in a reference to the independence of Cuba, Spain's last major colony, in 1898. The movement was characterised by a self-reflexive mode, seeking to redraft a modern 'Spanish' identity in a post-colonial context. In stylistic terms, a restlessness of form focused on trans-generic experimentation, direct engagement with readers by way of a conversational style, and the investigation of inner states through stream of consciousness and interior monologue. A robust prose was sometimes rippled by allegory, in plots tossed about by an existential lack of closure. All of this resonates with O'Brien, whose work also features the most notable characteristic of the '98' group: an obsession with the arid endurance of the land of Castile, as somehow symbolic of a utopian Spanish character. O'Brien's character Agatha Conlan—austere, direct, introverted, conflicted—exemplifies the temperament of the '98 Generation, including a love of Castile (see O'Brien, 2000a: 214; O'Brien, 1962a: 32, 46). Castile is a houseguest in *My Ireland* and *As Music and Splendour*—where it is mentioned in passing—and it sits in judgement in *Farewell Spain*, *That Lady*, *Teresa of Avila*, and *Mary Lavelle*—where it is associated with the moral centre of the book. This is the view southwards onto the plain:

> Roofs of dwelling-houses, the river; acacias and bushes of rosemary. Roads, ash-white, hardly discernible against ash-blond fields. Thin poplars, groups of farms. Empty, golden, harvested land. Strips of long shadow, movements of flocks. At the remote and dreamy edge the snowy mountain-heads. Above a speckless and incomparable sky. Nothing that can be held in dramatic words; nothing sweet, nothing emphatic. Simply a view worth a thousand journeys and which one hopes to keep in recollection always. (1985b: 119)

The very sparse prose, bone-dry here, takes in the humble shapes before us. The refusal to embellish, to *re-write*, is a carefully measured aesthetic choice. It is an example of the best writing of the '98 group.

Existentialism

Kate O'Brien's work falls within the coordinates of existentialist fiction. Most of her novels are about characters whose pre-ordered lives are derailed when an unprepared-for choice presents itself. In a public lecture on literature, O'Brien claimed that the existentialist writer and philosopher Jean-Paul Sartre had been for years "the leading European *Avant-Gardiste*", only to add in brackets: "(not in the *art* of writing, not at all, but as a moralist, and as a fearless censor of social thought, a director of society)" (emphasis in original, UL, Kate O'Brien Papers, doc 157: n.p.). Few have claimed that Sartre's novels made a stylistic, *artistic*, contribution of note, because his thesis-driven fiction requires a pared-down writing. But this is in itself an aesthetics, as O'Brien herself notes, after comparing the twentieth-century Jean-Paul Sartre, best known as a philosopher of individual freedom, to the eighteenth-century Jonathan Swift, best known as a satirist, praising, as we have seen, his "pristine" prose (ibid). This unexpected Sartre-Swift axis is revealing of O'Brien's position, which sees writing as always an aesthetic endeavour, and suggests an interesting literary 'genealogy' for her work.

Plotting is also a technical matter. Existentialist novels do not accrue information; they have a point to make, so lyricism and elaborate writing would be a distraction. Nor do they follow a traditional three-partite structure of 'set-up, confrontation, and resolution'; their narrative peaks are unrelated to action, and have to do with an ethical challenge, with anguish, with realisation. An example is this *climatic* moment towards the end of *Pray for the Wanderer*:

> Matt felt inert, unable to take his usual part in the table-talk. The effort to control anxiety had induced along his nerves a flow of irrational sadness which blurred his wits; a defence mechanism which kept his mind from full panic … And the inertia of sadness increased, became heavy as foreboding. … Irrational, self-pitying – but deadly sorrow. A farewell heard only by the self. A knowledge of inescapable change. (1951: 145)

Section Two: affinities

Beyond O'Brien's stated or traceable allegiances to a number of movements, she had an affinity with various aesthetic perspectives. These cover a remarkably wide range, featuring ostensibly contradictory modes. The traditional mislabelling of O'Brien's style as an uncomplicated, regressive, functional realism, does indicate a display of realist markers. Melodramatic elements, and important references to the Burkean sublime, are two other pre-modernist narrative and emotive affinities which are relevant. Perhaps on the opposite side of the aesthetic spectrum, we find strong markers of conceptual art, reminiscent of 'pure abstraction', with O'Brien for example deploying stark structural designs, appealing to the intellect only. Finally, lesbian aesthetics is a key perspective, present in both individual interventions and an overarching sensibility.

realist

Kate O'Brien once referred to "that illusion of life and truth which is the function of literature" (1943: 8). Her work is invariably placed by critics within realism. Assuming that modernism is a kind of 'deep realism' which seeks to capture life as it happens, she can be considered a *bona fide* realist. Consider how she captures a snippet of conversation overheard in a tram in "Singapore has Fallen" (of 1942, uncannily similar to Elizabeth Bowen's "Unwelcome Idea", of 1941). Much of O'Brien's work is set in pre-modernist times, but how she looks at nineteenth-century opera singers in Italy, for example, is not how a Victorian writer would; leaving aside the main theme of young women's affective-sexual *apprentissage* (an erotic and sentimental education) in stylistic terms her structure, plot lines, and point of view are modern. O'Brien's narratives rarely take flight away from clarity, when she is describing a setting, an action, or a thought. Also, pointedly against modernist practice, she insists on giving detailed backgrounds for all her main characters. Information accumulates, for example by the inclusion of full letters, a convention of nineteenth-century realism. Every corner is covered, every issue dealt with, where a full-blooded modernist would have stepped back, refusing to disentangle all threads. Within orthodox literary criticism, a writer must be either realist or modernist, yet O'Brien does not conform to that division.

O'Brien was determined to be understood, and the popularity of her books suggests that she maintained efficient communication channels with her audience. A twentieth-century development of realism, socialist realism, sought to use fiction to promote socialist beliefs. Clarity of exposition was the key tenet of socialist realism, because those books had an urgent message to convey. As we will see later, O'Brien was an activist writer, therefore it was imperative for her to communicate clearly—see the light conversational tone of *Farewell Spain*, a book written in earnest and haste to encourage support for the losing side in a war—but her multiple agendas sometimes sat uneasily together. She spelled out the ethical conundrums her characters face, and those characters often declare their communism, atheism, lesbianism, in quasi-didactic fashion. However, no realist writer would have produced the bullfight-sex scene in *Mary Lavelle*, the dream-like atmosphere of *The Flower of May*, or the mock-confession scene in *As Music and Splendour*, which are examples of surrealism.

melodramatic
There is another mode of narration which helps contextualise O'Brien's narrative strategies, often resonating with nineteenth-century writing: the melodramatic mode. Her plots often feature the startling discovery, the crushing disappointment, the heroic endurance, the manoeuvring by relatives. We are thrown into tales of damnation, of love-as-suffering; we witness dramatic entries and exits; we listen to declarations of forgiveness, declarations of war, and to dying words. Byronesque heroes (Matt in *Pray for the Wanderer*) and heroines (Mendoza in *That Lady*) make a stand.

Heart-broken characters break down in tears (Denis in *Without My Cloak*) or join a convent (Helen in *The Land of Spices*). All of these features attest to a deep knowledge of, and affinity with, the melodramatic tradition, of particular resonance in the English theatre. Emma Donoghue has suggested that "melodramatic dialogue" is a strategy used by O'Brien to reveal the outmoded masculinity of certain characters, such as André in *The Flower of May* (2009: 21), but O'Brien's interest in melodrama is more widespread than that.

The focus of her characters' internal monologues is the elucidation of *feeling*, rather than the almost-scientific pursuit of the essence of *thought* that we find in other modernists. Yes, there is a gallery of intellectually-rigorous, unswervingly-logical, emotionally-detached characters in O'Brien, from Clare Halvey to Agatha Conlan. Yes, there is also a 'will to understand', in O'Brien's ethical challenges and her plea for tolerance of difference. But her stories always seek an emotional involvement from the reader. Stylistically, this translates to a baroque quality, an excessiveness which may partly account for the perception of something "misshapen", to borrow Fogarty's word, in O'Brien's work (1993: 101).

conceptual

Unexpectedly, O'Brien also shows a strong affinity with conceptual strategies (rather than an allegiance to conceptual writing), in the shape of structural design, conceptual use of language, and what we may describe as cognitive interventions. In terms of design, her novels are often built from the centre outwards, through a 'hinge' event. In *The Land of Spices*, the hinge is the protagonist's recollection of a shocking discovery in her youth. *The Flower of May* offers an extreme example, with two distinct halves modelled on the operations of a lighthouse, in order to radiate change. The hinge event can shift the genre, as in *Mary Lavelle*, where the unexpected apparition of Juanito at the exact physical centre of the book, shifts the *Bildungsroman* into a romance—a perilous stunt which resulted in the mislabelling of the novel as a text-book Romance.

In terms of conceptual use of language, in *As Music and Splendour*, for example, 'to sing' is meant to be read in parallel as 'to sin', so that the musical training of the protagonists stands for their erotic development, to elude censure and liven the reading experience. As for cognitive interventions, an interesting example from *The Flower of May* is designed to activate the part of the 'cognitive map' in the reader's brain which stores certain associations: "the tower of St Mary's", "the immaculate morning sky", "three swans in sail", and the lily-like Lilian, with her "white-ruffled neck" (1953: 186–7). This is *more* than symbolism, it seeks to saturate the mind with the colour white, and *disable*, by saturation, the hypocrite Lilian's display of purity, a virtue traditionally associated with white.

Burkean sublime

Kate O'Brien's affinity with the Burkean sublime can be traced throughout her work. In a treatise of 1757, Irish philosopher Edmund Burke identified the Sublime as a more interesting and valuable category than the Beautiful, as something compelling and overpowering, a source of astonishment, "with some degree of horror", associated with "vastness" (53, 124). Taking up this cue, O'Brien described the period between the Spanish revolution and the fascist coup, 1934–37, as "a death, or a *vast*, unpredictable birth" (emphasis added, 1985b: 36). Also in Burkean mode, in *Mary Lavelle* O'Brien claimed that to the neophyte, an appreciation of the harsh land of Castile, or of the Spanish bullfight, is "suspect and savage", with the bullfight described as "[b]urlesque, fantastic, savage", and also "an immense thing" (2000a: 215, 116, 140).

In thinking of sex, Helen Archer conjures up a "dreadful" image, "vast or savage or gargoyled or insanely fantastical" (2000b: 158), while Juanito and Mary are "grotesquely and harshly made one"

(2000a 309), and a man confessing to his lover that he is a priest is met with "[t]he distortion, the grotesque, the inferno!" (2005: 342). In the 1980s, philosopher Julia Kristeva developed the idea of the Abject: something that is repulsive and familiar at once, and therefore elicits a particularly conflicting form of rejection. The Abject shares an ambivalence of perception with the Sublime, but not its superior value; had the Kristevan reading of abjection been available to O'Brien, she would have found it congenial. O'Brien is very interested in investigating and dismantling Beauty as cultural construct, a project she shares with Edmund Burke. As we will see later, she furthered that philosophical project by contributing 'shabby' as a category of intrinsic value, superior to both Beauty and the Sublime.

lesbian aesthetics

Kate O'Brien has an affinity with lesbian aesthetics, understood as a place of connotation and contestation which stresses female embodiment and female experience, and seeks connections to an often muffled or tentative tradition. For example, there is a lesbian significance to many of O'Brien's favourite, amulet-like words: 'nature' (from Radclyffe Hall's *Well of Loneliness*), 'heavenly' (Ulrich's redeployment of Plato's queer 'Uranian' love; see Robb, 53), or 'genius' (a Wildean code for homosexuality). In terms of a lesbian literary tradition, O'Brien models her lesbian Clare and attendant Evans on Woolf's Clarissa and gay double Septimus (in *Mrs Dalloway*, of 1925), she gives Agatha the paleness, height, "hungry loo[k]" and "mobile ... mouth" (2000a: 85) of vampiric lesbian precursors Carmilla (in le Fanu's story "Carmilla", of 1872) and Christabel (in Coleridge's poem "Christabel", of 1816), and gives Luisa Areavaga in *Mary Lavelle* the golden eyes of bisexual Paquita Valdez (in Balzac's novel *The Girl with the Golden Eyes*, of 1833). A lesbian sensibility also bursts through O'Brien's heterosexual scenarios, for example in *The Last of Summer*, where the sexually inexperienced Angèle expresses her desire for Tom, who has given her a gift of a shell from Carahone beach, thus: "She ran her mouth along the smooth lip of the shell" (124).

Lesbian aesthetics and erotics are aligned by O'Brien in Anna Murphy's epiphany at the end of the woman-centred *The Land of Spices*. We find a consistent index of lesbian sensibility in the importance of the female touch, and hands "hold a special place in O'Brien's body language", as traced by Emma Donoghue (see 2009: 17). In stylistic terms, the sheer wealth of subtextual and fictional autobiographical interventions may be O'Brien's greatest contribution to the literature of lesbianism. Connotation is not just necessity, but a fun game too, and a giddy complicity is also part of lesbian aesthetics. Consider the description of Nell in *Pray for the Wanderer*, who has an air of "Madame du Deffand ... he thought mischievously—or Saint Catherine of Siena. Or some might have said Sappho" (1951: 13).

Section Three: influences

O'Brien's work was influenced by art and literature in important ways. The influence of the arts extends from painting, music, and cinema, to so-called 'minor arts' such as gardening, interior design, or fashion. She reclaimed bullfighting as an art, taking her cue from Hemingway. A connoisseur of bullfighting, this "controversial" activity (O'Brien, 1985b: 206) was given by O'Brien as an example of "art, unconcerned and lawless" (2000a: 117). In the visual arts, painting is of particular importance. Music is a key referent, from popular dance music to opera. Cinema, particularly the *avant garde* of the first half of the twentieth century, also made an impact on her writing.

arts

In O'Brien novels paintings give additional information on a character, or force a character to confront a difficult idea. When paintings appear on the walls, they signal a correspondence with the person using the room. For example, "an oleograph of a young woman with a palm branch in her hand" (2005: 1; *As Music and Splendour*, signifying Saint Catherine) alerts us to forthcoming lesbian sacrifice, a reproduction of *The Burial of Count Orgaz* (*Mary Lavelle*) alerts us to a doubling of the character who owns it, or an original Fragonard (*Gloria Gish*) predicts a diversion at a high personal cost. In other occasions, painting plays a pivotal role, as in the "battered volumes of old master reproductions" (2000b: 272) which prove an education to the future artist Anna Murphy, or a deep dislike of El Greco, through which Juanito and Mary signal their heterosexuality to each other.

"I am influenced by the singing voice and by dance music", O'Brien explained in *Self-Portrait* (RTÉ, 1962). Her in-depth knowledge and understanding of the operatic tradition resulted in the insightful and skilful composition of *As Music and Splendour*. Classical opera offers a display of heightened emotion in often melodramatic plots, it has female protagonists, and it is structured through arias that facilitate the expression of intimate thoughts and feelings. All those features can be found throughout O'Brien's work. An extremely popular artform in the nineteenth century, opera also facilitated the expression of lesbian desire, through the ambiguous 'trouser roles' (male roles designed for a female voice and played by a woman performer). The greatest of them all, Orpheus, is made great use of by O'Brien, who thus places herself in a tradition reaching from Gluck-Calcabigi's 1762 opera *Orfeo ed Euridicie* to Sciamma's 2019 film *Portrait of a Lady on Fire*. Elsewhere, 'ordinary people dancing' in public squares (*Mary Lavelle*), sisters longing to sing to each other *(The Ante-Room)*, or religious hymns marking the rhythms of convent life (*The Land of Spices*), break up the narrative to let feelings rush in.

Cinema is an important influence in the fiction of O'Brien, who as we know had once attempted to become a professional screenwriter. Her nods to *avant-garde* cinematic techniques are particularly impressive. German expressionism is a salient referent, with O'Brien applying its lighting effects of heavy contrast between light and shade, or use of anti-realist spotlights, mastered by directors like F.W. Murnau, in novels such as *Mary Lavelle*. Her script for *A Broken Song* features dream sequences with superimposed images, characteristic of early surrealist films by pioneers such as Germaine Dulac. O'Brien's novels feature camera pans, zooming, and closeups, as well as a distinctly cinematic fast editing, efficiently used in fragmented memories, for example, in Helen's reaction to seeing her father and Etienne in *The Land of Spices*. In *Pray for the Wanderer* Tom likens his mind to a film camera, declaring that his aim as a novelist is to show "[t]hat life is so and so on *the screen of my closed eyelids* ... I give you life translated to my idiom" (emphasis added, 1951: 184).

Other artforms are also important in O'Brien, from the established fine arts, to garden design. The latter is particularly relevant in *Without My Cloak*, where Denis in fact "formulate[s] a philosophy of gardening" (1987: 46), but also noteworthy in *Pray for the Wanderer* (see 131–2)—at a time when it was not yet considered an expression of individual aesthetics. She also made a case for bullfighting as a misunderstood art form. O'Brien had a keen interest in architecture, and it plays a particularly important role in *Mary Lavelle*, with buildings used as metonymy, a 'substitute' for Agatha (the Renaissance church of San Vicente), or to symbolise the central romance (the Romanesque chapel of "The Holy Angels"). Interior design and fashion are used by O'Brien for characterisation, but in terms of aesthetic strategies, it is more relevant that she regularly uses colour to bind scenes or indicate affinities; for example, the blue-white colour scheme in Luisa Areavaga's apartment is carried over to the Madonna's robes in the statuette that adorns the room of governess Mary, signalling a deep connection (see Mentxaka 2011: 124–25). This is an intermedial exercise in painterly writing.

literature: twentieth century

In terms of literary influences, most of the relevant figures are near-contemporaries whose careers had peaked around fifteen years before her own emergence as a novelist. Among twentieth-century writers, Joyce, Woolf, Hemingway, and Proust are important referents. Among writers of the nineteenth century and earlier, Emily Brontë, George Eliot, and Austen are traceable in O'Brien, as well as the Russians, and the French Naturalists. She admired many writers, but their influence is not necessarily discernible, Beckett being a case in point.

O'Brien once declared that "James Joyce is my man. Here is a writer who tells the truth about himself" (1963: 46)—neglecting to mention that she was quoting an obscure line from W.N.P. Barbellion's diary (see *English Diaries and Journals*, 46). Elizabeth Foley O'Connor has claimed that Joyce is O'Brien's "most sustained and pervasive literary mentor" (2014: 11). O'Brien paid homage to *Ulysses* in *Pray for the Wanderer*, where the novel is described as "the most awful outcry ever raised about the powers of darkness" (71; see 59–60), but the most important outcome of the influence is *The Land of Spices*, "Kate O'Brien's portrait of the artist as a young woman" (Dalsimer, 1990:59), modelled on Joyce's *Portrait of the Artist as a Young Man*, which is "echoed at several points" by O'Brien, as first noted by James Cahalan (1988: 208, 217). Ann Owens Weekes has described the intervention as "revisionist" (1990: 128), but there is no question that respect and admiration are part of the mix.

The work of Virginia Woolf was a key influence on O'Brien's later work. *As Music and Splendour,* for example, features a grafting of *Mrs Dalloway*'s plot, and an experimental section (the five friends' Roman dinner) modelled on Woolfian prose. O'Brien designed an entire book to pay homage to Woolf, her 1953 novel *The Flower of May*. A puzzlement to critics (see Tighe-Mooney 2014: 273), its very structure and set of characters are a literary experiment. A series of memorable characters created by Woolf are recognisably 'reincarnated' in *The Flower of May*: Eleanor Pargiter, Rhoda, Mrs Ramsay, and Orlando become Fanny, her aunt Eleanor, and her mother Julia. Stylistically, a conceptual binary structure of light-dark builds on Woolf's central symbol in *To the Lighthouse* (see Mentxaka, 2018: 136–39). In a sense, the exercise also represents an 'Irishisation' of Woolf—as Sharon Tighe-Mooney has shown, the new 'Mrs Ramsay' represents "Mother Ireland and a past that is no longer relevant", while the lighthouse is itself a symbol of the nation (2014: 280, 275).

O'Brien was also very alert to the work of her contemporary Hemingway, who shared with her an interest in Spain and the Basque Country, in leftist politics, and in challenging sexual mores—including an unexpected commitment to (mostly) positive lesbian representation. In a review of 1937, O'Brien criticised Hemingway's "sloppiness" (quoted in Walshe, 2006b: 70), but in terms of aesthetics, his famously direct, conversational style, chimes with O'Brien's. In their non-fiction, both writers often speak in an over-assertive tone, displaying their 'connoisseurship', a characteristic of a certain type of journalistic reportage. Appropriately, O'Brien discussed Hemingway in *Farewell Spain*, but his influence is most notable in *Mary Lavelle*, where she built the structure of the romantic plot as a spectacular intertextual experiment, entwining her novel with Hemingway's description of the acts of the bullfight in *Death in the Afternoon* (see Mentxaka, 2011: 92–100)

O'Brien's admiration for Proust was partly related to his queer valence, and his narrator's comments on the homosexual "freemasonry" of underground, secretly-connected comrades (as described in *Sodom and Gomorrah*; see 21), are paraphrased more than once in her work. In stylistic terms, Proust interested her for his efforts to show how layers of time and experience are interconnected. As O'Brien put it, Proust, together with Turgenev, "taught us that the memories we sit down to, that we select and seek, are false" (1962a: 6). That is, we all fictionalise the past. O'Brien's pageant of autobiographical characters is one of her greatest contributions to literary creativity. O'Brien enjoyed playing with temporality: she presented the same self simultaneously at different ages, interacting in the same book (Juanito/Pablo Areavaga in *Mary Lavelle*), or in different books and times (Denis Considine /Thomas Evans in *Without My Cloak* and *As Music and Splendour*). But her characters often feel "weariness and sadness" from an awareness of 'making memories'—of the passing of time (as we learn in *Mary Lavelle*, 2000a: 248).

literature: nineteenth century and earlier

It has been argued that nineteenth-century fiction provided the main influence on O'Brien's work. Dalsimer referred to "[h]er traditional literary style, far more akin to that of the Victorian novel than that of contemporary *avant-garde* fiction" (1990: xvii). Hannah Sheehy Skeffington saw O'Brien as "[t]he Irish Galsworthy" (quoted in Walshe, 2006b: 69), and Elizabeth Bowen saw her as "the Balzac of Ireland" (quoted in Hogan, 1985: xi; but see O'Brien's dismissal of Balzac in *My Ireland*, 121). I place her work among that of her contemporaries, but she felt a strong empathy with some earlier writers, and admired others without wishing to emulate them. For example, O'Brien believed that George Eliot had "led the English novel ahead of itself in the nineteenth century" (ibid, 40), but Eibhear Walshe notes that the two novelists' ethical landscapes are markedly different (2006b: 117).

O'Brien's governess novel *Mary Lavelle* inevitably dovetails with *Jane Eyre*, in the protagonist's beauty as a negative of Jane's plainness, the 'Rochesterisation' of Don Pablo, and the personification of Eyre/Eire as a woman yearning for autonomy (see 2000a: 27). And yet, it was Emily Brontë, and not Charlotte, who O'Brien described as a true "genius", highlighting her stylistic abilities as a "poet" writing in prose, to refer to the historical mark left by her "burning shadow" (1993: 11). Jane Austen is one of Mary Lavelle's favourite authors (*Emma* is read by her charges, see 2000a: 178), but her influence is mainly important in stylistic terms, as the third person free indirect style she developed is O'Brien's most common point-of-view, allowing her to hover between inner and outer expression.

Three different traditions were also influential on O'Brien: 'The Russians', 'The French', and 'The Spanish'. O'Brien, who delivered radio talks on Gorki and Gogol, was particularly interested in Turgenev, as we have seen, on account of his technical approach to time. A graduate in French literature, O'Brien often cross-referenced the French classics–in terms of style, she prized a modern poetic turn, highlighting that: "with Flaubert [the French mind] recognises quite unselfconsciously the melancholy potentialities of a cab in a rainy street; with de Maupassant it smiles at a fat little feminine hand on a café-table" (O'Brien Papers, UL, doc 134: 12). But Jane Davison concludes that ultimately, "it is Spain that drove her aesthetics, not France" (2017:12), as shown by the influence of Benavente, Cervantes, and Teresa of Avila on her work. An affinity with Benavente's plays, as Davison shows, is implicitly attuned to modernist priorities, as both writers' work is "open to a reading as a social commentary as well as an exploration of the human psyche" (ibid: 45).

PART III: LITERARY STRATEGIES

Section One: modernist stylistic patterns

Kate O'Brien's most original contribution to literature, in her aesthetic practice rather than her admittedly ground-breaking themes, may be in her interest in layering and intersecting meanings. O'Brien's main preoccupations are psychology, the (temporary) truth of the subject, and politics. Her technically rich narratives work in tandem with her content. There are two main sets of literary strategies in O'Brien's work: the modernist-infused strategies, and the purely O'Brienesque ones. In terms of modernism, her approach includes interventions on plot structure strategies, point of view strategies, and intermediality. In terms of O'Brienesque literary features, they generally correspond to an aesthetics of connotation, including the use of significant words, allegory and personification, intertextuality, subtextuality, and intratextuality, and an interest in encoded life-writing.

plot structure

Kate O'Brien's plot structure strategies seek, in modernist fashion, to avoid the traditional realist linear progression that corresponds to a certain understanding of life, action, the self, and readerly comfort. Generally, her strategies serve an existentialist model of continuous change, a focus on the inner truth of a character, conflict between overt and covert narratives, and a lack of closure. O'Brien is committed to a structural anti-linearity of plot. Her stories favour *inner* motion: a transformative journey, professional development, from disconnect to connection, an ethical dilemma. Overall, in Kate O'Brien novels very little happens externally, and whatever action we witness, has the function of triggering a chain of reflection in the characters. In modernist fashion, they are driven by thoughts, not deeds.

In her anti-linearity, she favours three types of structures, which often co-exist: a hinge in the middle, two parallel stories, and surface-submerged stories. When a key event is revealed in the middle of a novel, as we have seen, it shifts the story, the mood, and sometimes even the genre. When a double story is embedded in the structure, it can be a double-track where the melody is carried in turn by one character or the other (Clare and Rose in *As Music and Splendour*, Matt and Tom in *Pray for the Wanderer*), or a 'then-and-now' simultaneity with multiple temporalities (Agatha-Nieves-Mary in *Mary Lavelle*, Helen as girl-Helen as woman in *The Land of Spices*). When a submerged story runs below the surface, it can carry political meaning (e.g. an apocalyptic subtext in *Mary Lavelle*) or revised characterisation (e.g. the lesbianised Luisa Areavaga in *As Music and Splendour*). The refusal of a satisfying closure (in *Mary Lavelle*, *Pray for the*

Wanderer, or *Without My Cloak*) is another modernist feature exercised by O'Brien.

point of view

Kate O'Brien's approach to point of view is also modernist, as she uses stream of consciousness, free indirect style, interior monologue, and a 'double readerly location'. O'Brien's favoured narratorial point of view is that of the modernists: free indirect style, also known as free indirect discourse or *oratio obliqua*. In it, the narrator hovers between the character's point of view (first person) and the reader's point of view (third person). Ostensibly irrelevant thought processes are allowed to flow, under a lightly-arched discursive bridge, as in the following:

> Mary switched her thought with deliberation to the evening ahead of her. She must dine, she supposed, with Doña Cristina and Mademoiselle [after arriving in Madrid]. Depressing prospect. But as the meal would not be served until half-past ten, and as it was now not long after eight, perhaps she might go out – to a cinema, or to walk by the lake in the Retiro [park]. Or perhaps she had better not. The two old ladies may be scandalised. Better stay in, write a letter, and cause no trouble. She moved unhappily in her chair. She was really afraid of solitude nowadays, especially when it came swift on the heels of exhilaration. She wished she could go out again. How absurd a life! (2000a: 225)

Throughout O'Brien's work, we are met with the undiluted thoughts of characters in *oratio obliqua*, which adapts, by way of grammar, rhythm, and word choice, to specific character traits or specific moods. The short and stumbling staccato sentences of a distressed Caroline Considine (see *Without My Cloak*, 1986: 148), for example, can be contrasted to the long and meandering sentences that capture the girl Anna Murphy's reverie (see *The Land of Spices*, 2000b: 171). The action-free chapter 'Anguish of the Breast' in *Mary Lavelle* is an experimental showcase of modernist point of view techniques, focusing on a single character, Don Pablo, whose progressive anguish is matched by a stylistic progression from traditional point of view, to *oratio obliqua*, to stream of consciousness (a stream of thoughts without narratorial input), to direct expression of thought (see 315–25). Another point of view technique used by O'Brien is the doubling of 'readerly locations', an intervention on the reader, who is expected to bring together information from two interlocked texts, in a kind of pre-internet hypertextuality. O'Brien employs this strategy in both intertextual and intratextual links, such as the voices of Anna Murphy and Stephen Daedalus in *The Land of Spices*, or the distorted repetition of the bullfight scene from *Mary Lavelle* in the sexual encounter scene in the same novel.

intermediality

Another stylistic feature of O'Brien consonant with modernism is her interest in intermediality. She often mixes artistic mediums, not by referencing or evoking various artforms, but by merging some of their technical characteristics with her own writing on the page. Modernism was developed in cross-fertilising artistic communities, and an intermedial sensibility can be traced in many writers. As we have seen, Cézanne's paintings were the first to show that beauty "can lie in a rumpled table-napkin, and a half-empty glass" (O'Brien Papers, UL, doc 134: 12), a new focus on the small and the unimportant, which arts like literature and cinema then followed. O'Brien's intermedial experiments range from architecture to film. For example, she borrowed and adapted the use of light in German expressionist cinema, relying on strong lighting effects. This is a stylistic flourish, because lighting is unnecessary in strict literary terms. Here is an example from *Mary Lavelle*: "She leant against the tree, and looked at the figures moving in beauty through the violent depths of light. ... There was a white, hard light streaming in on her obliquely" (2000a: 189). In the same novel, we find an extraordinary example of intermediality using the film editing technique of double-exposure, with O'Brien superimposing the protagonist's face on that of a bull in the ring, by repeating descriptive details (see ibid: 304–7). *Mary Lavelle* also offers what may be the most stunning example of an intermedial application in O'Brien, in her use of the traditional structure of bullfighting, in three 'tercios' or acts, as the building blocks for the entire Mary-and-Juanito romance narrative (see Mentxaka, 2011: 90–100).

Section Two: O'Brienesque connotation

The O'Brienesque style is mainly an aesthetics of connotation, featuring layers and intersections. It may be that this is a literature of the closet. Lilian Faderman pointed out in 1995 that 'the literature of lesbian encoding' has been almost universally neglected (see 1995: 441–446), and this is still the case. In the words of Graham Robb, discreet literary suggestions were the "rhetorical equivalents of the inconveniences suffered by gay men and women in daily life: communicating with nods and winks, changing the loved one's gender for the purposes of conversation, pretending to share jokes about sexual deviance" (2003: 215). In this section, we will look at specifically O'Brienesque stylistic features in her aesthetics of connotation. These include the use of 'significant words', her use of allegory and personification, her interest in intertextuality, subtextuality, and intratextuality, and finally her career-long commitment to encoded life-writing.

signposting/significant words

O'Brien uses 'significant words' (to misappropriate art critic Clive Bell's concept of "significant form"; see Bell 1914: 8), either as loaded terms in themselves or for signposting a parallel narrative. Examples of specifically queer connotation include the description of Mary in the sex scene as "a wounded San Sebastian" (2000a:

309), a reference to a traditional gay-male subject, the homoerotic representation of the saint's martyrdom. O'Brien's insistence on Saint Teresa's "peculiar ... genius" (1993: 10) is also a queering strategy, as the word genius, via Wilde's claim that "along with genius goes often a curious perversity of passion and desire" (2002: 42), can serve to mean 'homosexual', so O'Brien used "genius" to signpost Teresa's lesbian tendencies. Often certain turns of phrase are meant to signal to the reader that something else should take up their attention. For example, at one point Mary Lavelle claims that someone believes they saw "my double in the plaza San Martin" (O'Brien, 2000a: 200). That is a way of alerting the reader to the fact that a (rather complex) duplication process is at play in the novel.

allegory and personification

Kate O'Brien's interest in a layering of meanings, makes her adopt personification and allegory. Personification is typically used to reflect on a given country. For example, we are told in *Mary Lavelle* of Mary's childhood dream of 'perpetual *self-government*' (2000a: 27), a strange turn of phrase. Given that Mary now lives in the Basque Country, seen by many as a stateless nation, and that she is twenty-two years of age at the time the novel is set in 1922, this indicates she is a personification of an Ireland that is finding her feet. In *The Last of Summer*, published in 1943 but set in 1939 before World War II breaks out, the matriarch Hannah Kernahan is a personification of a different Ireland, symbolising de Valera's isolationism and his particular brand of authoritarianism. These associations facilitate allegorical narratives, with Mary-Ireland falling in love with Juanito-communism to investigate the viability of such union, or Hannah-Ireland keeping Angèle-Europe at bay to elucidate the egotism of neutrality.

intertextuality

Intertextuality is another O'Brienesque feature. Anne Fogarty has referred to her "eclectic web of intertextual references" (1993: 104). Her cross-referencing is remarkably complex, and a number of her books in fact make of intertextuality their *raison d'être*. As we have seen, if *The Flower of May* pays homage to Woolf's work, *The Land of Spices* reworks Joyce's *Portrait of the Artist as a Young Man*, echoing it at crucial points, as in this reworking of Stephen Daedalus' 'girl on the beach' epiphany, into Anna's consciousness:

> Now, however, she saw Pilar in a new way. She became aware of her and of the moment on a plane of perception which was strange to her [and] saw her, it seemed, in isolation and in a new sphere, yet one made up of broken symbols from their common life and which took its light from the simplicity of shared associations ... [so that this] foolish school-girl [became] an exquisite challenge to creativeness; she saw Pilar as a glimpse, as if she were a line from a lost immortal; she saw her ironically, delightedly, as a motive in art (2000b: 271–2).

As we have seen, Jane Davison has studied a web of intertextual links between the work of Jacinto Benavente, Cervantes' *Quijote*, and the figure of Teresa of Avila, and several O'Brien characters. All of O'Brien's novels are peppered with intertextual touches, so for example Henry Archer's lover is named Etienne, just like the beloved mentor of the Renaissance thinker Michel de Montaigne, Étienne de la Boétie. Montaigne, who claimed for their "union" a "complete fusion of the wills" (1993: 97, 99), offered an appraisal of the Greek erastés-eromenós model in his essay "On Friendship". Another telling example is the suggestion that the presumably heterosexual Mary Lavelle had been "in love with love" (2000a: xvii). This is a typically O'Brienesque example of subtextual acrobatics seeking to disrupt normativity, here through a reference to the homosexual excesses in Saint Augustine's youth in the fourth century, as related in his *Confessions*: "in love with loving", he had succumbed to Sodom's "monstrous tides of foul lustfulness", although before his repudiation of the past, he admits almost coyly, that "[v]erily all desire joy" (1966: 32, 33). In *The Land of Spices*, the child Anna gets hold of the *Confessions* to the alarm of a nun, a hint of the revelations to come in the novel (see 2000b: 113).

subtextuality
Subtextuality is a particularly O'Brienesque strategy because she is a master of it. It may be that women writers have a particular affinity with the technique, as Elizabeth Abel, Marianne Hirsch, and Elizabeth Langland have noted that "[t]he tensions that shape female development may lead to a disjunction between a surface plot, which affirms social conventions, and a submerged plot, which encodes rebellion" (1983: 12). Queer literature, as we have seen, is also amenable to subtext, and we see the technique put to good use in *Mary Lavelle*, which offers an encoded lesbian *Bildungsroman* (Nieves-Mary-Agatha), as well as the first chapter of a lesbian romance narrative (Mary-Luisa) that will reach its conclusion in *As Music and Splendour* (Clare-Luisa). Nieves is the girl Mary was seven years before, and Agatha is the woman Mary will become in fifteen years time, and the characters' relationship is a figurative meeting of past and future selves (see Mentxaka, 2011: 25–27).

Subtext, as this example shows, is sometimes facilitated by the use of a *Doppelgänger*, a double. This technique, associated with modernism but predating it, is one of O'Brien's signature techniques. There is no novel by O'Brien which does not feature *Doppelgängers*. In *Pray for the Wanderer*, Tom and Matt are one, as their mirroring names suggest, representing the adjusted and the misfit. In *The Ante-Room*, the rivals Vincent Regan and William Curran are in fact mirroring doubles, two equally unviable conceptions of love. In *As Music and Splendour*, the classical interpreter Clare Halvey is divided (as the name suggests), with the modernist composer Thomas as her alter ego—and we may take this to be an allegory of O'Brien's own conflicting aesthetic interests.

intratextuality

Another O'Brienesque feature is her intratextuality, or 'autotextuality', that is, the criss-crossing of references internally within the author's work. All of her novels are interconnected, either by links between characters (e.g. the protagonist of *The Ante-Room* was a side character in *Without My Cloak*), by plot lines that present variations on a theme (e.g. Agnes in *The Ante-Room* is a version of Mary Lavelle saying 'no' to an extramarital affair), or by autobiographical trails (e.g. in *Distinguished Villa* and *Without My Cloak*, as her first novel's Christina is a variation of her first play's Guildchrist, two versions of the same experiences). O'Brien's approach to intratextuality does not envisage a progressive finessing of characters or plots as her career advances, but a back and forth movement where related character types, and a modified central plot, dance in different permutations to similar songs played in slightly different tempos.

We find an interesting example of intratextuality in *Farewell Spain*, which gives additional information on *Mary Lavelle* in such a way as to create a virtual third space between the two books. For example, in one instance, the travelogue describes the river Ibaizabal as "mobile" (1985b: 208), an unusual term which the earlier novel had also applied to *the mouth* of the character Agatha, who lives near its bank (see 2000a: 87). There are no accidents in O'Brien. This is a metonymic intervention, one of a series of confluences designed to emphasize the fact that Agatha is a personification of the compelling and unforgiving city where she lives. There are multiple other examples in O'Brien's work.

encoded life-writing

The most remarkable O'Brienesque stylistic feature may be her commitment to encoded life-writing, which resulted in a gallery of printed portraits and self-portraits spanning the period between 1926 and 1958. Interestingly, O'Brien's only book of literary criticism was a book on life-writing, *English Diaries and Journals*. In it, she pays close attention to suggestions of non-normative sexualities. It could be that her autobiographical writing had to be encoded to protect her, at a time when her lesbian sexuality would not have been acceptable. Yet we see an interest in fictionalising lives which exceeds that context, as her work includes several portraits of, for example, her beloved sister Nancy 'Nance' O'Mara and her mentor Dr Enrique Areilza.

O'Brien was driven by her belief in the fictional character of memory, and by extension, of the self resulting from the accretion of experience. As Eibhear Walshe has noted in *Kate O'Brien: A Writing Life*, O'Brien gave several key characters the same age as herself at time of writing, and in doing so she left a visible trace of her intentions (for example, see Walshe, 2006b: 84). She wanted her self-portraits to be identifiable, as we see from another feature, her giving the striking blue 'Thornhill' eyes she had inherited from her mother, to characters such as Agatha Conlan, Fanny Morrow, or Clare Halvey. She also sealed her meandering transformations with riffs on the same name, from Lavelle, to 'Nell Bell' to 'Clarabelle'. Kate O'Brien's aesthetic practice thus extended to reimagining, or replaying, her own self.

CHAPTER 3:

SEXUALITY & AFFECT

PART I: AFFECTIVE

affective bonds

This chapter offers a discussion of the complex affective and erotic fictional worlds in Kate O'Brien. Her work's representation of sexualities and affects covers relationships, acts, and feelings which either conform or do not conform to existing social norms, here referred to as normative and non-normative. Typically, in O'Brien's stories, the pull to conform and the pull to break free are wrestled with by a young female protagonist who will grow up as a result of this internal conflict. She faces a choice, which suddenly makes visible the intricate workings of right and wrong she had not noticed before. If she steps into a proscribed choice, she will fall into the crushing social machine, temporarily clogging it.

When tracing the affective map of Kate O'Brien's novels, plays, and short stories, we can start by distinguishing non-erotic affective bonds of love and affection from romantic love. Friends, relatives, classmates, and colleagues sustain the development of her protagonists. Falling in love, on the other hand, almost always trips them up. O'Brien makes the intersection between love and sexuality either unexpectedly complex or an irrelevance. Her books are famous for their focus on transgression, but the transgression is often love, which can be more interesting and more problematic than sex for O'Brien. Within marriage, love is the covenant, as we learn from a young priest in *The Land of Spices*: "to let yourself love another person more than the one you had promised to love best always—that is adultery" (91).

While O'Brien surveys the Victorian romantic ideal with a satirical eye in *The Ante-Room*, she puts her full weight, as a writer, on demonstrating the power of love and affection to test growth and to mould humane women and men. It is striking, however, that affection, desire, and intimacy rarely converge in O'Brien's work. One of her greatest contributions to our understanding of identity may in fact be her thinking on love as the key to sexual orientation, as we see below. Most of her protagonists start out alone, and slowly build affective bonds. The emotional and social map of her novels is dominated by friendship—often between siblings or in 'sororal' attachments—as well as mentorship, and romance. Love is "an expression of life's latitude and possibilities" (1951: 123), and O'Brien explores neglected paths and inaugurates others.

(falling in) love

In Kate O'Brien, love is both a threat and a bounty. It introduces itself as a problem, as "[t]he malady of love" (2000a: 51). Characters invariably fall in love with the 'wrong' person. Love is a threat to an individual's psychic coherence and to civic cohesion, because it is transformative. It makes characters grow up, emotionally, psychologically, ethically, and politically. It is revolutionary, and can heal the "wounded and self-wounding world" (1981a: 34). Love may be partly 'produced' through the romance discourse in literature—O'Brien satirizes it through the Victorian Vincent in *The Ante-Room*—but, ultimately, as we learn in *Pray for the Wanderer*, "romantic love is not an invention so much as a discovery, like America or radium" (1951: 123).

Love is sometimes used as a strategy by O'Brien's characters, invoked as a musical baseline to sex, so that it carries the melody. It is more difficult to object to sex if it simply 'follows' feeling.

Agatha declares her love to Mary Lavelle, and the women's bond strengthens, because both *love* unrequitedly. Churchgoers "see[k] mercy, explanation, and forgiveness because they are so vicious as to love each other" (2000a: 285–6). Yet, in *As Music and Splendour*, O'Brien also suggested that an 'affective orientation' is unrelated to sexual behaviour. Luisa's male lover Duarte declares that she "has never been in love with me … And indeed it would have been wrong and grotesque had she been", because Luisa is lesbian (2005: 296). Kate O'Brien here disassociates the traditional pairing of love and sex, presenting love as the true indicator of orientation, a radically original way of thinking about identity in 1958.

'familial'

'Familial' groupings are central in all of Kate O'Brien's novels. Affective bonds can be articulated through communities, biological or non-biological. Mostly, families feature as a unit that protects the group but does not sustain the individual. Biological families band against intruders in *Without my Cloak* and *The Last of Summer*, as do professional communities, from the nuns of the (ironically named) '*Compagnie of the Sainte Famille*' (tr. Company of the Holy Family) in *The Land of Spices*, to the 'Café Alemán' governesses in *Mary Lavelle*.

But it is often after the failure of, or neglect by, formative homes that protagonists make their own families as best they can, or drift into them: *vide* Helen Archer's nuns, or Clare Halvey's circle of musicians. The unconventional Lavelle, Conlan, and O'Toole eject themselves from the governess' community to create a family within a family, as do Caroline and Eddy in O'Brien's first novel, a 'family saga' about the Considine clan, where the emphasis falls on exclusion from the family rather than on mutual support.

There is an important exception to the shifting notion of the familial in O'Brien, and that is her treatment of sisters. Though sometimes unfathomable (*Gloria Gish*), treacherous

(*The Last of Summer*), or both (*The Flower of May*), they are as often dependable and loyal to the point of self-obstruction (*The Ante-Room*), projecting their love onto the next generation and quietly shielding young nieces—such as Mary Lavelle and Fanny Morrow—financially, through their wills.

friendships

The most common affective bond in Kate O'Brien is that of a pair of friends, generally two young women, whose deep connection will be unaffected by the circumvolutions of their individual lives. Some of these friendships in fact read as improvements on familial bonds, as ideals-come-true, and appear to us bathed in an almost unnaturally perfect aura: Rose and Clare (*As Music and Splendour*), Lucille and Fanny (*The Flower of May*), or Matt and Tom (*Pray for the Wanderer*) seem forever united, before and after we meet them. Unlike them, protagonists who start their journey alone, yearning for a connection, do not always find it. In *The Last of Summer*, Angèle arrives in Ireland friendless, and leaves still friendless. In *Without my Cloak*, Denis ends up getting more solace from his garden than from the people in his life. In *Mary Lavelle*, the protagonist is lonelier as the train leaves Altorno than she was when she arrived.

In O'Brien's work we also find friendly lovers, who are affectionate, supportive partners, without the encumbrance of love, such as the lovers of Ana de Mendoza, Rose Lennane, or Luisa Carriaga. Conversely, friendships sometimes evolve into passionate attachments: little Anna Murphy's erotic awakening as she observes her schoolmate Pilar, or Agatha's realisation that she desires her friend Mary, or Clare and Luisa's falling in love onstage as the friends (ominously) sing the leads in Gluck's *Orfeo ed Euridice*.

self-reliance

Kate O'Brien's heroines and heroes are self-reliant. This is not always by choice; it is sometimes the arrow in their ethical compass, and they stubbornly choose 'loneliness' over surrender to unethical arrangements (the adolescent Mary Lavelle's "main idea had been to be free and lonely"; 2000: 27). We find an extreme example of this when Ana de Mendoza refuses to appease the King of Spain and is forced into permanent house arrest, reminiscent of a live burial, like a modern Antigone. Making choice an imperative for her freethinkers means that most of O'Brien's protagonists end up alone *after* tasting what lasting companionship may be like.

Through O'Brien's use of the *Döppelganger* motif, two halves of one person often sound a note of self-love. In *The Flower of May*, the relationship between Fanny and Lucille has been described by Reynolds as "a true emotional bond, an *amitié amoureuse* in which [either girl] has as much to gain as she has to give" (1987: 88). They can also be seen as two halves of a person divided by the demands others place on her, a person further doubled in Lucille's brother Patrice, who is in love with Fanny. We find the exact same arrangement in *As Music and Splendour*, in the relationship between the singer Clare Halvey and her double, the composer Thomas Evans, who is in love with Clare. Thomas may be a wink at the 'Narcissus' narratives of homosexual development (eroticising sameness by reworking the myth of Narcissus, who fell in love with his own reflection in the water), but his final assessment of the lesbian Clare, with a mock-Catholic absolution of sins (see 2005: 156), is a moving declaration of self-sufficiency.

pedagogic

Another important bond in Kate O'Brien, transcending but incorporating affection, is the pedagogical relationship. Mentoring is considered in close detail in *The Land of Spices*, where the bond between the convent's Mother Superior, Helen, and the child pupil Anna offers sustenance and support. In the same novel, little Charlie becomes a feminist after informal conversations with the suffragette Miss Robertson, in an encounter presented as 'a pedagogical event.' O'Brien sometimes reverses the traditional roles, with Milagros Areavaga becoming her governess' unofficial teacher in their meandering walks and facilitating Mary Lavelle's awakening to philosophy and politics.

Pedagogical partnerships are sometimes inspired by the classic Greek *erastés-eromenós* model, which some scholars refer to as the pederastic model, and incorporates the theme of carnal knowledge, as we will see later in more detail. This is illustrated in the professor of literature Henry Archer, who has at least two relationships with male students. More surprisingly, we find an echo of it in *Mary Lavelle*, when the older Don Pablo is stirred by the "Greek boy" quality of Mary (2000a: 67), and takes her under his wing (and, through his double Juanito, becomes her lover). This developmental model is implicitly a non-binding, temporary bond, with fewer expectations or demands attached, as we see in the loose arrangement between Rose and her teacher-lovers Antonio and René in *As Music and Splendour*.

PART II: GENDER

Gender intersects with sexuality, and O'Brien exploits the intersections to wake the reader to a range of deviations from the normative. O'Brien's female characters challenge rules on sexuality so spectacularly that their contestation of gender norms is easy to miss. It is not necessarily that O'Brien's interventions on gender are subtler, but critics and readers are diverted by the cultural weight of sexuality, and the make-or-break effect of legal censorship so closely associated with O'Brien's career. It can be argued that at its core, gender is more important than sexuality in the two-tier patriarchal system, as its most visible aspect in an unequal society where public behaviour is more strictly monitored than private lives. Femininity and women, traditionally bound together, are dislodged from one another by O'Brien in order to question what Gayle Rubin calls the "sex/gender system" (1975: 159). O'Brien's deliberate and systematic obfuscation of gendering is a characteristic of her work. In this section we look at some aspects of her representation of femininities, masculinities, androgyny, and transgender markers.

femininities
Denis Considine's devotion to garden design—a pastime still strongly associated with women in 1934—Juanito Areavaga's "gentle step" (2000a: 300), or "the lovely manners of a Jesuit" displayed by Matt Costello, (1951: 61), in *Without My Cloak*, *Mary Lavelle*, and *Pray for the Wanderer*, are all traditionally expressions of femininity. Femininity is associated with gentleness, passivity (or, in de Beauvoir's formulation, the immanent and "static", 108), and beauty. The defining characteristic of Mary Lavelle (a play on *la belle*) is not her extraordinary beauty, but her indifference to it. She connects with the world at deeper levels: intuitive, emotional, sensual, or ethical. This trait is underlined in many other characters, from Tom Kernahan, who is "as beautiful as Apollo and Gary Cooper" (1989: 124), to "Clarabelle" Halvey (2005: 73) and the "weary and beautiful" Eleanor Delahunt (1953: 217), in *The Last of Summer*, *As Music and Splendour*, and *The Flower of May*, and is one of the most interesting and innovative aspects of O'Brien's work, as it queries the traditional value ascribed to beauty.

O'Brien contests the notion of woman as externality, be it adornment or muse. She does not discard the perception of beauty, as a right, as a human achievement, and writes women who are agents or aroused observers. Luisa Areavaga's elaborate gender presentation, for example, may be an exquisitely refined "female masquerade", the concept popularised by Joan Riviere (1989: 35), but her studied simplicity is also a sign of intelligence, a substantive trait, because she pleases herself first. Her appearance is an arrangement which has more of artistic expression than of gender compliance. O'Brien also bravely demands a female position of aesthetic appreciation, as in the justly famous scene where the Irish girl Anna Murphy awakens to beauty as an *experience*, while breathlessly staring at her Chilean-Spanish classmate Pilar at the end of *The Land of Spices*.

masculinities

We know that O'Brien's female characters are often assertive, understanding 'assertive' as self-expressive (rather than aggressive), even when they are being tentative, experimenting, or impulsive. This extends to the expression and pursuit of sexual needs or interests, but can by no means be restricted to it. Assertiveness is traditionally a gender trait associated with masculinity. We find the "reversal of the usual seduction scene", with a snatched kiss as "an expression of freedom, not of love", when Fanny kisses André Marie (Reynolds, 1994: 60, 108), and also when Christina kisses Denis, Mary kisses Juanito, or Agnes kisses Vincent. "'Do you know that you're seducing me?'", Juanito says (2000s: 306).

The range of genders available to men in O'Brien's work include various forms of masculinity. Consider the self-sufficient monkishness of 'spoilt priest' Paddy in *As Music and Splendour*, the perpetual cheerfulness of teacher Henry Archer (atheist scholar of religious poetry), or the predatory and manipulative Father Don Jorge, who uses his priest status as cover for sexual abuse. Here we have three characters with a religious background or interest in common, a feature often presented in fiction as a specific form of masculinity, whose gender identities could not be more different from each other. Some of O'Brien's characters can be seen as studies in 'female masculinity' (a concept first discussed by Suzanne Vega in an article of 1991). Eye-patched Ana de Mendoza, ugly Agatha Conlan, or "fat, plain" *Mère Générale* (2000b: 25) lack conventional beauty, which makes them less 'feminine'; by choice they are also self-confident, uncompromising, and reason-bound, all traditionally masculine attributes.

androgyny

Some characters in O'Brien have an androgynous quality. She regularly exploits gender ambiguity, as we see for example in her association of opera singer Clare Halvey with the 'trouser role' of Orfeo, her comparison of Mary Lavelle to Saint Sebastian, or her interest in nuns who use male names after consecration, as we see in *The Land of Spices* with, among others, Sister Thomas, "the shopping sister", Sister Simeon, "devoted to incubation", and Mother Mary Andrew, "erratic and cruel" (115, 127, 74). In *The Ante-Room*, Agnes Mulqueen's face is described by Vincent (later reprised as Don Pablo seeing Mary Lavelle) as "a boy's face and a woman's, the face of an archangel and of a lost little girl" (234).

An interesting strategy is the use of 'angelic' features, which can be traced throughout O'Brien's work, and is often (though not always) used to signal androgyny. Examples range from the protagonist of *The Last of Summer* Angèle Maury, to the poisonous beauty of a sexual predator associated with the fallen angel Belial in "Manna", to a series of 'angelic' characters in *Mary Lavelle*—an element which in fact inspired the title of this novel's film adaptation, *Talk of Angels*, taken from the way in which Agatha is introduced to the reader (in 2000a: 84; in deliberate O'Brienesque fashion, this is echoed in *As Music and Splendour*'s introduction of Thomas; see 2005: 140). Androgyny is most remarkably incorporated through the duplication of characters, in *Döppelganger* pairs with differentiated masculine and feminine traits. This is the case with 'feminine' Matt and 'masculine' Tom in *Pray for the Wanderer*, Mary and Agatha in *Mary Lavelle*, Clare and Thomas in *As Music and Splendour*, or Lucille and Patrice in *The Flower of May*.

transgender

A number of critics have suggested Agatha Conlan is a version of 'the invert', a transsexual, a man in a woman's body (e.g. Coughlan, 1993: 74, Donoghue, 1993: 42). Inversion, a concept developed in the nineteenth century, was considered an inborn condition, and often strategically used by gay rights activists to demand rights on the basis that it was a natural occurrence rather than a choice. Before the consolidation of queer theory, there was a tendency to confuse transgender and transsexual. Agatha Conlan reads newspapers and attends bullfights, because her 'masculine' (in 1922) interests emanate from her personality, not because she wishes to be a man. In the same novel, Don Pablo's library includes the work of Havelock Ellis, the key early theorist on inversion, and his daughter Nieves' "chief day-dream was that she was an English boy at Eton" (2000a: 16), so she could perhaps be seen as a genuine transsexual character. But it is worth considering that children in O'Brien, such as the child Mary Lavelle and Anna Murphy, dream of becoming explorers, doctors, guerrilla fighters, and those dreams are conditional on them being male (see ibid, 27; 2000b: 207). Theirs is a political, not a physical, conundrum.

The illicit sexual relationship between Ana de Mendoza and her lover has been described as "a covert meeting of transgendered lovers" (Walshe, 1993: 161). Sword-wielding, black-clad Ana, and her 'popinjay' Antonio are gender contrarians. It is in this sense that most of the significant characters in O'Brien, including those discussed above under the headings of masculinity and femininity, may be said to be transgender. She *does* seek to disturb and traverse traditional gender designations, and her characters' gender markers do just that.

PART III: NORMATIVE SEXUALITIES

norms

Kate O'Brien's work focuses on the non-normative. We need to establish what constitutes normative behaviours, feelings, and identities, before we establish what is non-normative. The normative refers to moral and legal understandings of what is acceptable in terms of sexuality. It is enforced, policed, and internalised in various ways, and it is subject to historical change. O'Brien's career developed within an English-speaking context, affected by the distinct legal, cultural, and historical characteristics of England and of Ireland in the mid-twentieth century.

The Irish context was one of Catholic fundamentalism, in a recently-formed Irish state noted for its isolationist and regressive policies. Protestant Britain, and cosmopolitan London in particular, were comparatively more progressive, but still not free from institutional censorship, legal enforcement of sexual behaviours, and the weight of Christian morality. Kate O'Brien, referring to sexuality in *My Ireland*, claimed that "one need not be engaged on Ph.D. theses on Love Customs or whatever to admit that Ireland has always taken its modest part in commission of the most attractive of known sins" (57). Be that as it may, Terry Eagleton has claimed that it is with O'Brien's fiction "that love and desire in itself and for themselves, irrupt into Irish literature in English in a major way for the first time" (2009: 97). Neither theme is unproblematically presented. In particular, as Eibhear Walshe has noted, "[t]he erotic in O'Brien is both liberating and, at the same time, destructive" (2018: 229).

The norms regulating our affective-sexual lives are such a dynamic aspect of social organisation, that they can be discussed from very different angles. This section will use marital status as the organising descriptor, understanding marriage as an artificially-set boundary which regulates civic obligation. Marriage is described by one of O'Brien's characters as "the great Illusion!" ([sic], 1951: 158). The fetishisation of marriage is crucial to the creation of "regimes of normal", in Michael Warner's formulation (1999: 16), and it is so ubiquitous in literature as to go almost unnoticed. O'Brien makes it visible. For example, in *The Land of Spices* a nationalist Irish priest in the first decade of the twentieth century, discusses why "[o]ur young girls must be educated *nationally* ... to be the wives of [middle-class] *Irishmen* and to meet the changing times!" (92, emphasis in original). Conversely, when O'Brien's characters decide not to marry, they are implicitly challenging the status quo. This is sometimes explicit too, as we learn in *Pray for the Wanderer* when Nell suggests to Matt, after he talks of marriage, that "[i]t would be braver and more realistic to take more casual comforts, and chance the draughts" (1951: 158).

married

All of O'Brien's novels feature loveless marriages. Many of them had started out as genuine love matches, but a gradual cooling down of passion had left no sustaining warmth. This is the case with Don Pablo and Consuelo in *Mary Lavelle*, Caroline and Jim in *Without My Cloak*, or Marie-Rose and Vincent in *The Ante-Room*. They sleep side by side, "[a] curious intimacy which the world called natural", but they know that "the life they led was not a love life" (2006: 136, 135). It is significant that in the period of O'Brien's career, divorce was not legal in Ireland (since 1922), Spain (since 1937), Italy or Belgium—the countries where her novels are set—so that here normativity is legally enforced. "In the Spain of which I will be premier", a frustrated Juanito says, "there'll be divorce" (2000a: 259).

Marriages of convenience also feature, lacking an erotic or emotional bond. Perhaps the most obvious example is the marriage of Reggie and his mother's nurse in *The Ante-Room*. He has syphilis, and she can provide companionship in exchange for financial security and status; their agreement is presented as a reasoned pact. In a number of cases, single characters seek a marriage that will ensure stability after a convulsive event. Irish peasant Christina in *Without my Cloak* is 'sent away' to the USA by Denis' wealthy relatives in Ireland, and she engineers a marriage with Mr Paren that will see her settled, and safe from opprobrium. Men seek 'convenient' marriages too, as we see in the case of Henry Archer.

Extra-marital affairs are the single most important plot-line in O'Brien, often entwined with a story of personal development.

Contemplating an affair is often presented as an ethical challenge, and as often the affair has disastrous consequences (consider the deaths of Julia Morrow and Pablo Areavaga), but in most cases the lovers—Ana de Mendoza, Mary Lavelle, Henry Archer— are unrepentant. In *Pray for the Wanderer*, we are told that "[a]dultery and homosexuality [are] entirely respectable so long as their practitioners [have] the *savoir faire* to keep them so", and are abided by "discretion" (O'Brien, 109). Caroline Considine in *Without My Cloak* and Gladys Woodford in *Gloria Gish*, defy the 'discretion rule' and leave their husbands to elope with their lovers, while Lillian Morrow in *The Flower of May* is not discreet enough. It this context, it is particularly relevant that some lovers do not demand fidelity, notably Clare Halvey in *As Music and Splendour*, while others behave as if marriage has not yet been invented—notably Mary Magdalen in the film script of the same name, and Rose Lennane in O'Brien's last novel (until her lover's impending marriage disrupts her Edenic set up).

In O'Brien's portraits of married couples, prostitution features occasionally. In her play *Distinguished Villa*, Gladys' husband pays for sex and then kills himself, and in *Farewell Spain* prostitution is presented with the cold eye of a documentarian in O'Brien's travels through the slums of industrial Bilbao, as a grim necessity for some women. But there is a sense in which the foundation of normative marriage is a form of exchange whereby the wife surrenders her body. Perhaps one of the reasons why Mary Lavelle could not envision a life with Juanito is that, for all his charm and passion, he is sexually selfish and unimaginative, and would be contented with a partner who "loved him and ... gave him sensual peace", since he equates marriage, for a woman, to a job paid for in "bed [and] board" (2000a: 166).

unmarried

Among single characters in O'Brien, homosocial contexts are normative. Homosociality refers—via Eve Kosofsky Sedgwick's development of the term—to a social formation which encourages the close bonds between individuals or groups of the same sex, in a situation ostensibly free of sexuality, but in effect conducive to an erotic connection (see Sedgwick, 1992: 1–2). In the 1920s Bilbao of *Mary Lavelle*, the Café Alemán is such a formation, with governesses meeting up with colleagues, with eligible males and heterosexual romantic intrigues often discussed, but also facilitating lesbian attachments. Another example is the wave of same-sex crushes among school girls sweeping through a Limerick convent school in *The Land of Spices*—an adult lesbian is diagnosed with "delayed... Schwärm" by a psychoanalytically-inclined friend in *As Music and Splendour* (208). Yolanda González Molano has pointed out that O'Brien presents "a world of male homosocial relations" in *Without My Cloak*, in Martin, Joe, Tony, Denis, and Eddy, who form "a homosocial context which is only under threat by external forces" (313, 315, [my translation]).

A considerable number of O'Brien's characters are spinsters, bachelors, nuns, or priests. Many of her spinsters appear to be rather comfortable with their single lives, which suits their temperament and their way of life. Seen as eccentric or suspect, they are in fact settled, confident, even proud. Consider Aunt Eleanor, Miss Robertson, or Agatha Conlan—who is expected to turn with age into a "muttering hag", as she delightedly notes herself (2000a: 297). For some, however, spinsterhood is the only option. Agnes Mulqueen in *The Ante-Room*—after considering elopement with her brother-in-law, and a loveless marriage with the family doctor—settles for the perfectly normative choice of celibate singlehood.

The 'confirmed bachelor' was a Victorian metropolitan intellectual type which, in Sedgwick's words, "for some men both narrowed the venue, and at the same time startlingly desexualized the question, of male sexual choice" (1990: 189). A self-sufficient detachment is associated with a string of intellectually-inclined characters named Tom across various O'Brien novels. While

Victorian bachelors such as Dr William Curran in *The Ante-Room* see their status confounded by falling in love, a striking feature in O'Brien is that one time 'confirmed bachelors' such as Don Pablo, after marriage, somehow retain the aura of a loner, a self-contained older man absorbed by his own interests.

Life in a religious order is a normative option outside marriage. O'Brien is very aware that a mistrust of the body in general, and a phobia of sexuality in particular, are central to the outlook of Christianity. The moral discourse of Catholicism is sex-obsessed, and as a consequence celibacy is implicitly an 'ideal'. In *The Land of Spices*, O'Brien offers an extraordinary study of a nun whose decision to embrace the religious life was a retreat from the messy lawlessness of sexual passion, a normative option for Helen. The high status of Catholic priests and nuns in Ireland when O'Brien was writing was mainly due to the power of the Church as an institution. For nuns, the religious life was also a way of securing an education or advancing professionally, in managerial and teaching posts, and for men and women disinclined to marry, a safe life option.

PART IV: NON-NORMATIVE SEXUALITIES

nature
Sexuality has been legally regulated in most, if not all, societies, which suggests it is seen as problematic, a potential threat to social cohesion. So who may be said to be queer, to be outside the accepted norm? By queer we mean all "acts, identities, desires, perceptions, and possibilities" which do not comply with given societal norms (Butler, 1993: 228). Those norms, and therefore the non-normative or queer, are subject to a specific time and place. As Sharon Tighe-Mooney points out, O'Brien heroines specifically transgress "*Catholic* sexual boundaries" (2008: 128 [emphasis added]). During O'Brien's career, Catholic doctrine aggressively promoted sexuality as a goal-oriented activity geared

towards procreation (see the Papal encyclical *Casti Connubii* of 1930), so, in a Catholic country such as Ireland, any behaviour outside those parameters was *de facto* regarded as 'queer'. But in another sense, as Michael Warner put it, "to be fully normal is, strictly speaking, impossible. Everyone deviates from the norm in some way" (1999: 54–55)—and we could also say, with Sedgwick, that in a sense "sexuality, perhaps, can *only* mean queer sexuality" (1993: 20). In this section, we consider non-normative sexualities, beginning with LGB (lesbian, gay, bisexual).

"[F]or a novelist who was banned for obscenity", Eibhear Walshe contends, "she rarely depicts the sexual in her fictions and the few episodes of sexual love are disruptive" (2006b: 11). In Kate O'Brien's work, sexuality is perceived by most characters as being dysfunctional, a disabler of the normal, with the Rabelaisean 'beast of two backs' of penetrative sex described in a heterosexual context as "grotesqu[e]" (2000a: 309) and in a gay male context as "vast or savage or gargoyled or insanely fantastical" (2000b: 158). Lesbian and queer-heterosexual (i.e. non-normative heterosexual) longings are also likened to each other, as being "fantasti[c] and pervers[e]" (2000a: 296). Arguably, this is an activist strategy seeking to further lesbian and gay rights by making them 'relatable' to a general readership, by showing, as Clare put it in *As Music and Splendour*, that: "We all know the Christian rule—and every indulgence of the flesh which does not conform to it is wrong. All right. We are all sinners" (2005: 208). Gerardine Meaney has argued that "[p]rohibition and impossibility are the conditions of social existence in her fiction. O'Brien's novels are often ostensibly structured around the transgression or observation of a social or moral norm" (1997: 81). Her characters often see sex as a disabler of the self, but they know that the leap of making a transgressive choice is an existential validation.

O'Brien does not have much to say about sexual orientation in itself, since during her career this was not a freely discussed topic. As we have seen, she refers to homosexuality as "that peculiarity" in *Farewell Spain*, and also as an "accident" (146), which suggests an anti-essentialist approach. 'Accidental' is one of O'Brien's key words—which she applies variously to nationality, wealth, artistic ability, beauty, etc. Yet we are told of a character that "always she has been attracted to women" (2005: 296), a weighty 'always' which predates socialisation. We have seen in *Pray for the Wanderer* that "homosexuality and adultery were entirely respectable so long as their practitioners had the *savoir faire* to keep them so.... But tolerance and discretion were the passwords in regard to actual life." (109). Once again, a game of equivalences deliberately muddles moral rankings.

lesbian

Portraits of lesbians have often presented them as pathological, but in O'Brien being a lesbian is simply to "be in that love" (2005: 296). In an Irish context, after the fertile inspiration prompted by the Ladies of Llangollen, two historical women who eloped together in 1778 to set up a household in Wales and became celebrities for this transgression, and following the literary landmarks of Sheridan le Fanu's lesbian vampire in the 1872 short story "Carmilla", and George Moore's fanatic lesbian Cecilia in the novel of 1886 *A Drama in Muslin*, it fell to O'Brien's generation to offer more realistic portrayals of queer women whilst navigating severe state censorship. Elizabeth Bowen and Molly Keane took up the challenge, but O'Brien was the most committed, creating many powerful characters in stories brimming with equanimity and empathy: Anna Murphy, Clare Halvey, Fanny Morrow, Nell Mahoney, Agatha Conlan, Luisa Carriaga. The latter is a fascinating intervention: she is a version of a character from *Mary Lavelle*, heterosexual in 1936, 'lesbianised' in 1958: the golden-grey eyed Castilian Luisa Areavaga and the luminous-blue eyed Irish Lavelle, in love with the same man, are transmuted in *As Music and Splendour* into the golden-grey eyed Castilian Luisa Carriaga and the luminous-blue eyed Irish "Clarabelle" (2005: 73), now in love with each other (as discussed in Mentxaka, 2011: 25–28). Besides this intratextual rewrite, the two novels had independently expanded their lesbian content by using doubles: in *Mary Lavelle*, the lesbian Agatha is the double of the heterosexual Mary, and in *As Music and Splendour*, the homophobic Thomas is the double of the lesbian Clare (see ibid: 20, 75, 223).

Further, some characters become mouthpieces for a lesbian aesthetics and ethics, notably as we have seen in *The Land of Spices*, where a girl sees in another an eroticized aesthetic potential (2000b: 272). O'Brien's own women-centred novels are generally appealing to a lesbian readership. Many characters are independent from men, eccentric, outsiders, bright, quietly confident. Helen Archer, Aunt Eleanor, Miss Robertson, Nieves Areavaga, or Frances Lewellyn (in *Distinguished Villa*) are one hint away from being identifiably lesbian. As we have seen, O'Brien's biography *Teresa of Avila* is awash with hints, arguing that the reformer's (supressed) lesbianism was an important part of her makeup. Conversely, outspoken non-lesbian characters lauding reciprocal eroticism in the face of traditional lovemaking, such as Ana de Mendoza, are distinctly tuned to lesbian eroticism, in the emphasis on an assertive female sexuality and the expectation of reciprocity, both of which are non-normative in the period corresponding to O'Brien's career. In 1936, *Mary Lavelle* states that a heterosexual woman is expected to be "a passive and receptive thing" (2000: 57), and in 1958, *As Music and Splendour* has a lesbian assert that (in choosing to be a singer rather than a model) "'at least … I'll be doing the thing myself! Not just having it done!' (2005: 68). Lesbianism may be said to be O'Brien's plumb line when building her ethics of sexual satisfaction.

It is possible to get a little more specific. In a study of physicality in O'Brien that looks at her "language of embrace", Emma Donoghue has identified the prime importance of the hand in her body language, something consonant with lesbian experience as "the most expressive, flexible and tireless giver of sexual pleasure"

(2009: 23). The head is also important in O'Brien's work, for example in moments of "[s]troking or kissing the hair", and so is the kiss, a gesture generally "overburdened" with meaning which O'Brien includes, "not as the trite culmination of a courtship, but as a halfway marker, and often a tense one" (ibid 23, 24). Again according to Donoghue, when describing physical contact O'Brien favours certain words: "Her pet verb is 'stretch', her pet adverb is 'lightly', her pet noun is 'peace'" (ibid: 16). This three-part grammar itself offers a sketch of a satisfactory erotic contact.

gay male

The homosexual Henry Archer was placed as gently and surreptitiously as a cuckoo's egg in the nest of *The Land of Spices*. Despite referring with circumvention and elegance to the respectable and kind Henry and an ambiguously named Etienne, and despite taking utmost care to divert the censor's attention to the homophobic reaction of Henry's daughter, the novel was banned in Ireland for a single sentence: "She saw *Etienne* and her father, in the embrace of love" (2000b: 157). In her first novel, a "shabby" gay sculptor from Greenwich Village makes an unsuccessful pass at the co-protagonist Denis (1986: 387), and other queer men gravitate around him, including Martin Devoy and Eddy Considine (see Molano 312–21; Walshe, 2006b: 65, 52; Donoghue, 2009: 18).

Homosexual men hover throughout her books, many of them existing by virtue of connotation. For example, discrete references to 'Greek love' are a staple with queer-minded writers, and O'Brien is more refined and creative than most, as we see in Lavelle's "eccentric" uncle Tim (2000a: 226), who is a fan of the Renaissance painter Doménikos Theotokopóulos, better known as 'El Greco'. The wink should be even clearer to readers of Hemingway's *Death in the Afternoon* (extensively paraphrased in *Mary Lavelle*), where Theotokopóulos is anointed as "el Rey de los Maricones" (sic, Hemingway, 1960: 205); that is, 'King of Faggots". Unsurprisingly, O'Brien was an adept queer reader herself, as we see in her book of criticism *English Diaries and Journals*, which regularly excavates references to queer sexuality, such as the "eccentric" and "fussy bachelor" William Cole, whose journals suggest "a fair span of tastes and interests—as may be expected of a friend … of Horace Walpole" (1943: 22), or Katherine Mansfield and "her loves" (ibid, 46).

bisexual

In O'Brien, as is to be generally expected for mid-twentieth-century fiction, bisexuality is not invested in as an orientation in its own right. Its power to disrupt is exercised in a nominally heterosexual character's discovery of a homosexual kindling, without further concern for the new scenario. For example, the married Don Pablo in *Mary Lavelle* is suddenly attracted to a boyish girl, but there is no further soul-searching, while the widowed Ana de Mendoza in *That Lady*, frustrated in her intention to become a nun, falls in lust with an effeminate young man, in a gendered sexual twist which is not given further consideration. For most of his married life, *The Land of Spices*' Henry Archer has had affairs with men, but in the biography of the character scattered through the novel there is no attempt to elucidate his relationship with his wife.

If, as is customary, we equate sexual orientation and sexual behaviour, and bring in gender-variance and homosocial attachments as potential signs of non-exclusive homosexual tendencies, we find a number of potentially bisexual characters in O'Brien's work: Henry Archer, Pablo Areavaga, Ana de Mendoza, as well as Luisa Areavaga, Mary Lavelle, Denis Considine, Fanny Morrow. But the only *de facto* bisexual character in O'Brien is Luisa Carriaga, who in *As Music and Splendour* has one male and two female lovers. Alas, as Duarte explains to Clare, Luisa's identity may not be what it seems: "What Luisa thought she was doing when she made me her lover was to set up guards for herself" (296) against her own lesbianism. Carriaga's internalised lesbophobia means that she is in a sexual relationship with a man because she is "afraid" of her attraction towards women (ibid).

queer heterosexual
There are many ways of organising the wealth of O'Brien's representations of queer heterosexuality. Marriage is, as we saw earlier, an interesting grid, since married and unmarried characters have distinct needs and face distinct complications. As Anne Fogarty has pointed out, "O'Brien pointedly problematizes heterosexual identity" (2014: 157), both querying and queering it. Not only does she "us[e] queer moments to unsettle conventional views of femininity and to raise ethical questions about the marginalization of the subaltern", as Fogarty puts it (ibid), but her novels offer a remarkable portrait gallery of non-normative heterosexual characters demanding our full attention.

Marriage may be the epitome of normativity in terms of its cultural value as guarantor of status. In O'Brien, marrying can be a transgressive act, a badge of dishonour, a provocation, and, for society at large, a problem. Class-crossing and ethnicity-crossing marriages, for example, rattle the cage of the establishment. *The Ante-Room*'s Doctor Curran has little chance of marrying his social superior Agnes Mulqueen, and *Without my Cloak*'s Christina, a peasant engaged to the heir of the prosperous Considines, will be blocked out by his clan. In *The Last of Summer*, Angèle Maury is a French actor, which seems to present two insurmountable obstacles to an Irish marriage. But in *Mary Lavelle*, Rosie O'Toole, a 'respectable' Irish governess working in a foreign country, does marry a local Basque corner-shopkeeper, older and overweight, with whom she cannot communicate in words, and they bloom.

Marital infidelity, in the Victorian world O'Brien is bursting out of, may be said to be normative for men. There is no problem with the married Antonio's sexual involvement with Ana de Mendoza, but she must be punished for her transgression. Gladys Woodford's elopement is her downfall in *Gloria Gish*, Caroline Considine's fractures her family in *Without My Cloak*, and Lilian Morrow's extramarital affair is so horrid to contemplate that it precipitates her mother's death in *The Flower of May*. Therefore, we may say that the heterosexual women who break or ignore the marriage bond in O'Brien are *queer* within that historical period. Other marriages seem queer models of convivial understanding, with the heterosexual Catherine Archer in *The Land of Spices* seemingly accepting her husband's homosexual liaisons (if admitting that they should not have married; see 2000b: 139)—but as a woman, her acquiescence is in fact a normative response.

Some of O'Brien's queer heterosexual unmarried couples simply cannot marry. When it is not because of social barriers, there are legal ones. At a time without legal access to divorce in Ireland or Spain, some lovers have no choice but to face opprobrium and social death, and this was a sore topic in Ireland throughout O'Brien's career. In *Mary Lavelle*, political leader and lawyer Juanito may dream of a communist Spain where divorce is a given, and in *The Ante-Room* the Victorian Vincent may dream of leaving his wife to elope to the Aegean coast for a "paganly" life with Agnes (2006: 224); their inexperienced partners are more discerning—perhaps because they are younger, perhaps because they are women—and know the choice is between 'here, now, and be damned', or never.

Some of O'Brien's heterosexual unmarried couples do not wish to marry, which makes them queer by design, not by accident. Rose Lennane is perfectly content with a life of erotic dissipation, including a respectful but non-committal relationship with Antonio, until she leaves him when he enters a marriage of convenience in *As Music and Splendour*. It is part of the same erotic and sentimental apprenticeship that leads her friend Clare into an open relationship with Luisa. In *Pray for the Wanderer*, Tom Mahoney has been one such loose character, and the admission that he has an illegitimate child adds to his aura—free to marry, he never felt the need to conform, until Una crosses his path.

other queer formations

There are other queer formations, beyond the usual categories discussed in queer theory, which are important in O'Brien's imaginary. Incestuous attachments, the *erastés-eromenós* model, and a preference for celibacy among some lay people, are repeatedly visited, sometimes to add depth to portraits, sometimes as a character signature. Polyamory also plays a part, mainly in her last novel.

Incestuous bonds and feelings are relatively common in O'Brien's work. They involve a mutual commitment between two family members which overrides all other concerns, at times with an obsessive and possessive tenor, and regularly including an appreciation of physicality or an actual physical closeness and intimacy tinged with eroticism. The bond is particularly obvious in *The Last of Summer*, which uses the incestuous possessiveness of Hannah for her son as an allegory, in 1943, to examine the stranglehold of 'Mother Ireland' on any subject reaching for a continental connection. There are also multiple smaller references elsewhere—such as the presence of the "incestuous young Iago", a house cat in *The Flower of May* (192)—perhaps designed as normalcy disruptors. In addition to Hannah and Tom Kernahan, incestuous undercurrents define the relationship between Denis and his father in *Without My Cloak*, between Agnes and her sister, and Teresa and her son in *The Ante-Room*, or between Fanny and her father in *The Flower of May*. In O'Brien's biographical group portrait *Presentation Parlour*, she further points out how her aunt nuns were sisters "emotionally, even hysterically attached" (20001: 8).

The *erastés-eromenós* model was a template for homosexual relationships among cultured Greek men in the classical period. It was a teacher-pupil model, described in Plato's *Symposium*, whereby an older, experienced man, often married—the *erastés*—adopts an active role in a relationship with a young man in a passive role—the *eromenós*—(see Lewis, 1983). Sexual activity is here part of *learning* and socialisation. The textbook example is Henry Archer, "the Socrates of our suburb" (2000b: 143), in *The Land of Spices*. Further, the older Agatha begins the aesthetic and sexual education of Mary Lavelle, a crucial "first performance", by introducing her to the bullfight, so that "[Mary] was well initiated in one programme" (2000a: 117). Other bonds with a pedagogical component, read like sexless variations of the model. Youngsters are linked to an intellectually vibrant, unselfish older mentor, as with Helen Archer and pupil Anna, or Miss Robertson and her acolyte Charlie. Sometimes, a pair of similar age and background has one or both as 'teacher' to the other, as with Fanny and Lucille in *The Flower of May*, Tom and Matt in *Pray for the Wanderer*, or Caroline and Eddy in *Without My Cloak*.

O'Brien is enormously interested in and respectful of celibacy as an option, by religious and lay people. Spirited nuns are everywhere in O'Brien. The focus is on them in *The Land of Spices*, set in a convent school, in her biography of Teresa of Avila, and in *Presentation Parlour*, a bio-documentary about O'Brien's cloistered nun aunts. Interesting appearances include the gambling nun Jo in *The Last of Summer* or the rosary-wielding nuns likened to handball players in *Mary Lavelle*, but nun-like characters are even more intriguing, from Aunt Eleanor and her cigars, or Agatha and her books wrapped in brown paper "as nuns cover books" (2000a: 100), to the suffragette Miss Robertson, whose single status may have to do with the celibate pledge taken by some early feminists. As for priestly lay men, Paddy is moored in his celibacy, and Don Pablo has "withdraw[n]" into his (2000a: 62), reclaiming a sexual space that ensures peace and freedom. In *As Music and Splendour*, having "made [Iago Duarte] her lover", Luisa Carriaga then starts a relationship with Clare, and then has affairs with a number of women, including their common friend Julie Constant (296). When Iago warns Clare that their lover is "incapable of fidelity", Clare's answer is: "And are we in charge of her, Iago?" (ibid: 298). Such a response echoes Mary Lavelle's reaction after Agatha declares that her lesbian desire (for Mary) is a sin: "Oh, everything's a sin!" (2000a: 285). The defiance of social expectations in these two reactions, formulated as early as 1936 and 1958, is of enormous significance. Kay Inckle has discussed the radicalism of what she describes as utopian lesbian polyamory in O'Brien, in the context of a lesbophobic society where a double standard applies for 'fallen women' according to their sexuality (see 2007). While Clare is uneasy with a non-monogamous arrangement, she is compelled to respect Luisa's individual right to shape her own life. The novel's effort to eliminate connotations of sordidness and titillation in polyamory is remarkable: "To hear those polyphonic works with one's ears of flesh is a rest sometimes" (2005: 297), Iago declares.

PART V: NON-EQUAL & COERCIVE SEXUALITY

Non-equal and coercive sexuality are regularly occurring features in O'Brien's treatment of relationships. In the words of Alan Goldman, "[t]here is no morality intrinsic to sex", distinct from general morality (1977: 280). Most commentators seeking to identify an abusive scenario tend to focus on consent. While this is certainly a key element for assessment, it is useful to focus on reciprocity, to widen the scope. Not by accident, Ana de Mendoza refers to sex as "the whole art ... of *reciprocal* love" (1985a: 144, emphasis added). Perhaps half of the sexual encounters and relationships in O'Brien's work do not occur in full freedom, and many of them are undoubtedly coercive. In O'Brien there is a disturbing continuum between representations of rape and assault, and representations of normative heterosexual consensual sex, with consent more often than not muddled in the characters' perception. This remarkable situation is partly due to the fact that what is normative and what is non-normative is often difficult to determine in a world where, for example, women's subordination, or children's acquiescence, are normative. That is, the structural inequality makes it almost impossible to engage in a reciprocal, ethically-sound relationship.

mechanical

In a number of stories, sexuality is presented as mechanical, as an instinctual urge which, *for men*, requires no reciprocity. Such an understanding of sexuality is endorsed even by characters presented positively, whose assumptions are not contested. Juanito Areavaga, for example, declares to be contented with the facts that his wife "loved him and … *gave him* sensual peace" (emphasis added, 2000a: 166). Much has been made of the explicit sex scene between Juanito and Mary Lavelle, featuring an archetypal heterosexual sexual initiation which is painful for Mary, whose pleasure is sidelined. Critic Patricia Coughlan sees it as "a dismaying passage", which dwells "in an undeniably sado-masochistic way on images of Mary's specifically feminine vulnerability and pain *as themselves erotic* and constitutive of Juanito's pleasure" (emphasis in original, 69).

This infamous sex scene is in fact designed to mirror a bullfight, where in conventional terms (as described by Hemingway in the treatise quoted in *Mary Lavelle*) risk is less decisive than the will to engage. But it is also a *realistic* representation of a first experience of penetrative sex directed by an ordinary, ignorant man, who assumes the experience cannot be pain-free, let alone pleasurable, for his partner. The scene is therefore entirely normative, with sexual engagement understood as a self-serving male-directed activity. We also find this casual, naturalised arrogance in Vincent Regan, who came to marriage "furnishing it with his own dreams, and leaving no room for another's" (2006: 89), and in Jim Lanigan, a perfectly composed lawyer who, in his conjugal bed, is "no more than a beast in the country of love" (1986: 173).

abusive

Explicit sexual abuse and molestation feature a number of times in

O'Brien, suggesting a determination to put this issue—as she had done with many others—in the public eye. In *The Land of Spices*, it is implied that Mr Lawson is a paedophile who preys on children at the beach. In *The Last of Summer* we are told that as a young girl Angèle had been "surreptitiously petted" by an older male family friend (89). In *English Diaries and Journals*, O'Brien flippantly dismisses the nineteenth-century diarist Francis Kilvert's interest in young girls (see 1943: 42). In *Mary Lavelle*, the priest Don Jorge is a child-molester who makes implicitly sexual comments to the young sisters to whom he teaches music—when the girls' governess Mary finds out, she is at first unsure about reporting it, debating in her mind if she is fit to judge "right and wrong" (2000a: 133). This would be a striking development, were it not for the fact that lack of consent and lack of reciprocity are often treated with ambiguity in O'Brien.

While we have discussed the *erastés-eromenós* model as a queer formation within a consensual framework, the fact is that pedagogical relationships with a knowledge, status, and age differential need to work much harder to be egalitarian. Henry Archer's liaisons with his young male pupils are understandably 'suspect' because of the implicit vulnerability of his partners. In our times, they are not ethically acceptable. The fact that O'Brien follows up the Henry-Etienne scenario in *The Land of Spices* with a mentorship pairing between Helen and Anna devoid of any physical connotations, suggests that the two versions are being pitted against each other in a taxonomy of 'right and wrong' pedagogies, with Helen's literal distance leaving no room for abuse.

assault

There are some cases of sexual assault in O'Brien's novels. A casual reference to rape in *The Ante-Room* again demonstrates how certain proscribed behaviours can be normative in different contexts and at different historical times. When Vincent tells his sister-in-law Agnes that he could rape her, Agnes, who is in love with him, responds that his wife would be the only one "who'd get nothing out of the bargain" (232). This shocking exchange is a reminder of gender expectations in 1880, the time in which the novel is set, with assault being not only legally acceptable (in Ireland it was legal for a husband to rape his wife until 1990), but internalised as part of a gamut of acceptable behaviours. The sex scene between the loving partners in *Mary Lavelle* is dehumanizing and brutal, but it is not perceived by those involved as an assault.

"Manna" is the only unpublished piece of fiction which O'Brien took the trouble to copyright, and she possibly did so to authenticate the text for posterity. The story, which would have been unpublishable in 1964 and remains unpublished, recounts the sexual assault of the six-year-old Josie by a young man in the basement of a chemist shop. The title suggests a link to *Paradise Lost*'s Belial, a beautiful, graceful, charming angel who is in fact a deceiving demon (see Milton, 1900: 25/ Book I: 108–118). The reader is placed in the position of the child, registering and mirroring her confusion when an attacker snares a potential victim with a kind façade. Thus, Kate O'Brien offered in her fiction an unofficial and accessible archive, where the moral fog cast by abusers and with which survivors wrestle was made available to her readers. She documented non-reciprocal sexual relationships and acts, from normative conjugal relations to abuse and assault, at a time when few would speak of such things.

PART VI: GOOD SEX

Good sex is a rarity in Kate O'Brien—or so it would appear on first glance. All of her novels are concerned with the potential sexual misconduct of characters whose moral sense is unexpectedly challenged. Regardless of the outcome, O'Brien often focuses on the ways in which desire (generally as co-regent with love) causes personal and social havoc. Eagleton claims that "[d]esire in O'Brien's world is a kind of dreadful affliction, just as it is to Racine ... a kind of wayward, implacable force" (98), while, in the words of Emma Donoghue, "O'Brien's books celebrate passion-at-a-price; they are never anti sex" (1993: 183). In fact, not only is good sex to be found in her novels, but a number of characters are actively in pursuit of it—"pleasure was Ana's quarry", we are told in *That Lady* (65). We also find an *apologia* of sexuality as *apprentissage* (to borrow from Colette), an interest in "the redemptive role of the erotic" (Walshe, 2018: 234) and, everywhere, an appraisal of desire as a generative force.

(defining) good sex

Defining 'good sex' is somewhat difficult. According to Donoghue, in O'Brien "good sex [is] a bridge between flesh and spirit" (2009: 28). This seems to be corroborated by *Pray for the Wanderer*, where we are told that Louise and Matt are ideal lovers because of the "[s]heer, cold appreciation of each other's general make-up of character, mind and body" (85). But to Una, who is not in love with him or attracted to his temperament or his intellect, Matt has pure "'sex-appeal'", that is, "[h]e suggested a force which, once yielded to, would carry her far and deep in feeling", while Matt's ultimate assessment of Louise is that, "[a]s a lover, variable and moody as the sky, she could do no wrong. She was infallible"—and it is 'variability' that is the key here, rather than Louise's general make-up (1951: 162, 84). In *The Last of Summer*, Angèle "had heard people called sexual love a chemical reaction", and that is the only way she can explain her desire for Tom (124). Another key word, as we learn in *That Lady*, is "reciprocal" (1985a: 144). In O'Brien, we often find a definition 'by contraries', with unsatisfying sex or withdrawn sexual access being highlighted as an affront by a number of characters who are forced to retreat onto a sexless life. Unresponsive sexual partners within a marriage are relatively common in O'Brien—with particularly detailed accounts given by rejected parties Vincent Regan and Pablo Areavaga in *Without my Cloak* and *Mary Lavelle*. Marie-Rose Mulqueen and Caroline

Considine, in *The Ante-Room* and *Without my Cloak*, represent the other side, and their erotic withdrawal is a necessity.

In the case of Caroline's husband, the monstrosity of his sexual egotism is corroborated by her brother Eddy, a "*connoisseur* of love and passion" (1986: 173). Can it be an accident that this *connoisseur* is gay? In O'Brien, good sex is always non-normative, always proscribed – it has to be fought for, and losses are inevitable, generally in terms of social status. Ana and Antonio in *That Lady*, and (mirroring them) Rose and 'Tonio' in *As Music and Splendour*, are proud pairs of illicit heterosexual lovers, enjoying themselves mightily in the margins. Ana reflects:

> She was a sinner indeed, and at present shamelessly content to discover that she could in fact pursue the fabled pleasures of sexual intercourse to that point of irrational, participatory understanding and hunger which she had awaited legitimately in marriage, but which somehow then had just evaded her. Yet it was ironic to come to it illicitly at last. (1985a: 84–5)

Good sex is 'irrational, participatory understanding and hunger'. Variable, reciprocal, irrational, and participatory. Good sex is not a bonus, but a *right*. Whether they find happiness or not, it is not only justified but imperative that Doña Consuelo Areavaga refuse sex, or Mrs Caroline Lanigan leave her husband, because it is unacceptable that sex should not be good enough.

the art of sex (*apprentissage*)

The art of sex is compared to the art of music in O'Brien's last novel, *As Music and Splendour*, which makes a case for the gradual acquisition of sexual knowledge, by way of an extended allegory. At one point the co-protagonist Rose reflects that "Love, in many kinds, had offered her its education" (2005:132), but *apprentissage* is far more effectively addressed in the novel by making 'to sing' stand for 'to sin', and thus detailing how the trainee singers Clare and Rose become mistresses in the art of eroticism. That is to say, they become 'proficient and successful sinners', by learning to master their own voice range, gravitating towards the operatic roles best suited to their pitch, and finding the singing partner that complements their style and pitch. "[A]ccording to their natures, [the girls] spread and grew. They were lonely; they were lively—and they had, however unexplored and undefined, musical gift, musical need and desire" (O'Brien, 2005: 15).

Juanito tells Mary that she "must have patience. Love takes a lot of learning" (O'Brien, 2000a: 309). After her painful sexual initiation, when "the storm of feeling broke and took them again", the reader is told that "more and more her senses moved towards knowledge, and following her lover, she began to understand what love indeed might be" (ibid: 311). Mary does not learn it from her lover (she leaves him the next day), but Ana does from hers: "He had carried her a long way in pleasure; had taught her, late, the whole art in great and little of reciprocal love. Very gratefully she had learnt to count on her delight" (1985a: 144). Reciprocity is the touchstone—in fact it almost sounds as if it is the only thing that needs learning.

desire as gift

In O'Brien we find a formulation of 'desire as gift' (as we saw in the 'gift' of music). On the surface, a number of characters are eroded by passion, among them *Mary Lavelle*'s Don Pablo, whose long celibacy is tested by the attractive Mary, and Juanito, whose self-image is shattered by his extramarital affair: "I am undone", he declares (2000a: 307). But Pablo is in fact humanized by his desire for Mary Lavelle, and the same happens to the detached and monkish Agatha. This also applies to Natty in *Distinguished Villa*, suddenly and hopelessly enthralled by Frances. In the squared triangle of Agnes, Vincent, and Doctor Curran (with Marie-Rose as a mute participant) in *The Ante-Room*, all three become connected to the living tissue of the world when unwieldy desire unexpectedly appears, as it were, in their hands. Their isolation ends as they engage with their newly-discovered needs.

In *As Music and Splendour*, music becomes erotically charged, with loss (via Gluck's *Orfeo ed Euridice*) becoming a constitutive element of desire, even when reciprocated. As we have seen, 'the unexpected kiss' is a moment favoured by O'Brien which we find in many of her novels. This soft, non-threatening kiss, freely given in freedom, interrupts and deepens a moment of conviviality between two prospective, receptive partners who are already attuned to each other. Such a kiss is a gift, as bestowed by Christina, Agnes, Mary, Fanny. To these characters, desire demands to be expressed, even if it cannot be acted on. To them, desire is a superabundance of goodness, and the gifted kiss is an overspilling of that goodness.

CHAPTER 4:

POLITICS & ETHICS

PART I: ETHICS

'non-doctrinaire'

Kate O'Brien's novels are best known for pushing the boundaries of what could be said in fiction. In the words of critic Cathy Leeney, "[o]nly the crossing of a boundary makes that boundary visible" (2004: 150), and O'Brien's work shows the power of institutions and social forces to delimit individual growth and freedom. Her novels are a plea for tolerance of difference and dissent, which is in itself a political commitment. This chapter considers the relevance of ethics and politics to O'Brien's work, making a distinction between political fiction and activist fiction. In the first, we see various politics portrayed or reflected on the page, for example in the political beliefs or backgrounds given to a character, or in the references to the historical setting. In the second, we see an attempt to further certain political beliefs or delegitimise others. This chapter is thus organised in three distinct sections: ethics, politics, and activism. Fundamentally, politics is about how to live together, and it is in this sense that O'Brien's ethical books are political. "[P]olitics are death to the creative artist", Matt declares in *Pray for the Wanderer*, but only to add that if writers "must have a function, a social duty", then it is this:

> I believe that now as never before it is the duty of those who can refrain from meddling *not* to meddle. I believe that it is

useful at present to be an individual, to be non-doctrinaire.
I am not convinced about this, or prepared to be pompous
over it—but that may be the very *clou* of its usefulness.
(1951: 119, emphasis in original)

Kate O'Brien was steadfast in her "non-doctrinaire" mission, by providing debating and self-questioning characters. She also managed to engage very closely with political developments in Ireland, Spain, and the rest of Europe. In addition, she furthered a number of activist agendas, when she was ethically compelled to *act*, against her own advice, and took to the pen to enlighten, educate, and persuade.

locating Kate O'Brien's ethical dilemmas

Typically, a Kate O'Brien novel presents an ethical dilemma. In several plots, the female protagonist must decide if to embark on an extramarital affair, as in *The Ante-Room*, or to relinquish it, as in *That Lady*. In other novels, a character must decide if they accept a loved one's homosexuality, as in *The Land of Spices*, or one's own, as in *As Music and Splendour*. There is a tension between morality, which in O'Brien's world tends to mean Christian, specifically Catholic, morality, and ethics, which have to do with personal conduct and how one measures one's own needs and rights against those of others. Interestingly, a pedagogical impulse is discernible in the novels, which is itself a sign of an ethical commitment.

The ethics promulgated in O'Brien's work are specific: her writing explores an ethics of tolerance and reciprocity, an existentialist ethics, and an ethics of solidarity. In several instances, O'Brien characters find that transgressions have 'a morality of their own', a morality making its own specific demands at odds with prevalent views. Also, in line with the philosopher Santayana's view of experience, a sense of amorality can be felt by characters. Finally, O'Brien's work also presents a number of unresolved ethical quandaries, which may have to do with a 'sombre' fictional world which too often refuses satisfactory closure.

ethics vs morality

Kate O'Brien's work is saturated in Christian morality, specifically Catholic instruction. In her novels, the main conflict is not between individual and society, as in most *Bildungsromane*, but an *inner* moral battle. Christian morality is the recurrent handsome villain, attractive but poisonous—characters appreciate the clarity of the guidance, but are crushed by its demands. Considering that O'Brien was herself a non-believer, this persistent interest is remarkable. She was ambivalent about Christianity, which she considered in general terms a civilising force, as well as the crucial cultural binding element in European identity. Walshe has referred to "the enlightened, European Catholicism of her imagined bourgeoisie", which is an "invented version of Irish Catholicism" (2006b: 77, 86). As we have seen, O'Brien promoted the association of Christianity with a sense of Irishness and with a European identity, but she was also sorely aware of the conservative impact of Catholicism. Irish governesses in Bilbao in *Mary Lavelle*, for example, are intent on "ke[eping] their violent and terrible Irish purity" (2000a: 94). Violent and terrible, because its emphasis is on surveillance, and it is unforgiving.

Stray Irish Catholic Mary Lavelle, we have seen, notes caustically that Catholic churches are full of people "[s]eeking mercy, explanation and forgiveness because they are so vicious as to love each another" (2000a: 285–86), an obscene evolution of the central Christian message that "God is love" (John, 4:8). Most households in O'Brien have an "atmosphere of active Catholicism, decorum, taboo and self-discipline" (1951: 71), as described in *Pray for the Wanderer*. Her characters are forced to develop their own ethics in response to a morality that fails them, when "everything's a sin" (2000a: 285), as the protagonist declares in *Mary Lavelle*. The world proves too complicated for moral dictums, when a scholar of religious poetry (Henry Archer in *The Land of Spices*), a former novice (Ana de Mendoza in *That Lady*), or a mantilla-wearing, altar-cloth-embroidering Mass addict (Agatha Conlan in *Mary Lavelle*), are all 'damned' in the eyes of the church.

pedagogical impulse

Kate O'Brien's work is informed by a strong pedagogical impetus. It presents 'case studies' with backgrounds and outcomes that resist simplification, challenging the reader to condemn positively presented characters after having empathised with them. The objective, it seems, was not to persuade, but to undo moral certitudes. "We must train the young to think—not to learn, in their meaning of the word (though all thinking is learning)—but simply to think", O'Brien once declared, speaking to a group of university graduates in 1955, in a lecture titled "As to University Life" (5). Describing education as "the pursuit of truth", she specified a clause: "on whatever level or direction the pursuer seeks it" (ibid: 4).

The pushing of boundaries presented in O'Brien's fiction and drama can be seen as a pedagogy. And that pedagogical impulse can be seen as a politics. The link was made clear by O'Brien herself, when she stated in the same lecture: "We die, uneducated. But it may be, if we were careful, if we made notes, *if we wrote books*, that some vestige of the dust we raised might prove to gleam a little for the dustmen who follow us" (1955: 4, emphasis added). She hailed Plato's Academy as the ideal pedagogical space, "without other purpose than the furthering and purification of each [person's] thought. A place of argument, of silence, of perplexity, of back-and-overs" (ibid: 5). Thus, within the logic of this argument, O'Brien's work provided such a space, where rights and wrongs could be debated, and truths tested rather than imparted.

tolerance

The ethics promoted in O'Brien's work have particular

characteristics. They are an ethics of tolerance and reciprocity, as well as an ethics of the unfinished, and an ethics of solidarity. The value most often highlighted is tolerance, or the respect for diverse opinions, values, and ways of life. This translates into the O'Brienesque mantra 'Do not judge'. O'Brien does not over-rely on the Christian dictum of "Let the one among you who is guiltless be the first to throw a stone" (John 8.7), although it is implicit that an awareness of fallibility is an asset. In O'Brien, the emphasis is on 'judging' being *in itself* wrong. "Most people are [judges], indeed", she claimed in her sixties in *Presentation Parlour*, "[h]ardly ever does one meet [someone who isn't]" (62).

This single, exacting command is emphasised throughout the novels, and O'Brien employs every tool at her disposal to impress it upon the reader, including the (ethically dubious) use of unconscious association—a kind of writerly version of the cinematic 'Kuleshov effect', whereby contiguous images are selected to alter the viewer's perception. Thus, the paedophile predator in *The Land of Spices* is nicknamed 'the Judge' (see 2000b: 203), the conservative, inane but demanding fiancé in *Mary Lavelle* is referred to as "Mr Lawgiver" (2000a: 136), and the brutish, sexually selfish and ignorant husband in *Without My Cloak* is a lawyer by profession (ominously, so is the gentle Juanito Areavaga). An ethics of tolerance means respect, accepting all ways of life and all personal decisions which do not impinge on the common good.

ethics of reciprocity

An ethics of reciprocity is crucial in the ideological context of O'Brien's novels. It is particularly relevant in terms of sexuality, and O'Brien is very alert to how easily this asset is sacrificed when women are part of the equation. Even with mutually caring, devoted couples, we regularly find that the needs of women—and pointedly their *sexual* needs—are not met. When reciprocity is secured, female characters such as Rose Lennane or Ana de Mendoza are outspoken about it.

There is a peculiar, quietly significant moment in *Mary Lavelle* when, after a new governess treats her colleagues to cream cakes in a café, and one of them declines, this is seen as an unpardonable slip: "[G]ive the kid the pleasure of seeing you eat something", one declares, and the other replies: "How could that sight give her pleasure?" (2000a: 91). A gift must be honoured, and reciprocated in the *acknowledgement* of its value. Interestingly, there is no sense of this refined ethical stance being explicitly applied to blatant economic inequality. In the ethical roll call that is *Farewell Spain*, when a middle-class man responds to a beggar in a Bilbao street with "Forgive me, brother" (1985b: 203), this is interpreted as a sign of kindness, rather than hypocrisy.

an ethics of the unfinished

An existentialist ethics, which we can describe as an ethics of 'the unfinished', can be traced in the work of O'Brien. We have seen that in the 1966 lecture "Ireland and *Avant-Gardisme*", she described her contemporary the existentialist philosopher and novelist Sartre as the leading figure in European writing, "as a moralist, and as a fearless censor of social thought, a director of society" (O'Brien Papers, UL doc 157: n.p.). Choice, crucial to existentialist thought, is the crux of O'Brien's novels. Her characters do not have to learn to be free, but rather they must learn that *they are free*—free to choose. Once they discover that, they must coldly consider if they are to suppress their needs and comply with prevalent morality, or to prioritise self-actualisation and break the rules.

While O'Brien's approach to identity sometimes hints at core elements which remain unchanged—as for example in the sexuality of Luisa Carriaga in *As Music and Splendour*, of whom we are told that "always she has been attracted to women" (2005: 296)—there is a strong anti-essentialist strand in her work. In *My Ireland*, O'Brien claimed that "we ourselves, the travellers [in our life's journey], are never from day to day the same person that we think we know so well" (16). In her novels and plays, the self is often presented as an ongoing project. Her characters are always growing up, even as adults. The protagonist of *Mary Lavelle*, undergoing a new experience, becomes aware of "another, newer self" inside her (2000a: 116). Ethical rules must therefore make room for in-built change.

solidarity

An ethics of solidarity is also discernible in O'Brien's work. *Farewell Spain* was written and published at great speed in 1937 after the fascist coup in Spain, to try to gather support for the democratically-elected leftist republic among Anglophone readers. Solidarity also becomes particularly obvious in a group of novels contesting the non-interventionist stance of de Valera's government in World War II: *The Last of Summer* (1943), *The Land of Spices* (1941), and *That Lady* (1946). All are designed to comment on isolationism as self-obliteration, as cultural pathology. In "Irish Writers in Europe", O'Brien pointed to the Elizabethan consolidation of colonial power which ended eight centuries of Irish-European "scholars, priests, poets", when "the cable was cut and we [Ireland] were adrift from Renaissance Europe. A terrible loss" (1981b: 36). O'Brien's Europeanism sees neutrality as a dismemberment, a self-mutilation.

This also applies to characters who protect, accept, abet, or forgive transgressors on what appears to be the grounds of solidarity, arguing that they themselves have transgressed in the past. Again and again, we see characters who psychologically 'own' the transgressions of others, trying to understand their point of view. The philosopher Levinas developed a notion of empathy as a human trait, naturally triggered each time a new person or a new situation are faced (see 1981: 13). Considered in this light, Helen Archer, Mary Lavelle, or Ana de Mendoza respond kindly to the transgressions of Henry Archer, Agatha Conlan, or King Philip because of this form of O'Brienesque solidarity. It resembles an adaptation of Jacob L. Moreno's 'mirroring', a dramatherapy technique whereby one person responds to another by reflecting their stance, an "encounter" based on "total reciprocity" first theorised by Moreno in 1934 (quoted in Howie, 2014: 139–40; one of the influences on Levinasian ethics).

'a morality of its own'

Several novels point to amoral conduct which has 'a morality of its own'. The ethics associated with O'Brien's work are consonant with Henri Bergson's claim that "[w]e are free when our acts emanate from the whole of our personality" (1971: 129). Bergson went on to compare this dynamic to the relationship between "a work and the artist" (ibid), in a telling confluence between ethics and aesthetics. It is striking to see a similar idea presented in practical terms, for example in what amounts to an 'ethics of adultery' in *That Lady*. In this novel, the Christian Ana de Mendoza claims that "this love, this sin has a morality of its own that I find I understand" (1985a: 189). It is worth noting that 'this love' can be read here as 'this *type* of love' (much as Duarte refers to lesbian tendencies as "*that* love"; 2005: 296, emphasis added). The sinners find that they must sin in order to be true to themselves, an ethical imperative which takes precedence over social rules.

Ana is a key example of self-generated and self-regulated ethics, and the entire *That Lady* can be described as a debate on ethical self-determination. A powerful scene in *As Music and Splendour* culminates the career-long interest of O'Brien in individually-calibrated ethics. In a radical appropriation of the Catholic ritual of confessing sins to a priest to secure forgiveness from God, the double of the lesbian Clare, Thomas, approaches the bed where she is resting and says 'Ego te absolvo' ('I forgive you') (2005: 156). The scene is placed at the physical centre of the book—giving it structural weight, in O'Brienesque fashion.

amorality

Amorality is another feature of O'Brien's fictional universe. One of O'Brien's acknowledged influences, the philosopher George Santayana, valued Christian moral guidance despite being an atheist himself. But he contested the notion of intrinsically objectionable acts, shifting the emphasis onto the aftermath of an experience. In *The Sense of Beauty, Being the Outline of Aesthetic Theory*, Santayana claimed that a positive outcome is possible even if an experience is "evil", or triggered by an "ugly" event—defining ugliness as absence of pleasure—and declared that: "Truth is thus the excuse which ugliness has for being" (142). Such an approach shifts ethics from an action to its ultimate result, suggesting that behaviour is ultimately amoral. The idea is echoed in *Mary Lavelle*, with the protagonist declaring about a shocking, sickening experience that: "she had undergone it, which is all that matters about any experience" (129).

Sexual behaviour, its social regulations and the consequences of flouting them, is the main moral thermometer in O'Brien's work. As we have seen, Alan Goldman pointed out that if we define sexuality plainly as "the physically manifested desire for another's body", it is possible to conclude that "[t]here is no morality intrinsic to sex, although general moral rules apply to the treatment of others in sex acts as they apply to all human relations" (269, 280). In O'Brien, this becomes a dictum.

unsolved ethical quandaries

There are a number of unsolved ethical quandaries in the work of Kate O'Brien. For example, in *The Ante-Room*, Agnes must choose between her duty to herself and her respect for her sister, and there is a sense in which someone must always be punished when an ethical conundrum presents itself. In *Mary Lavelle*, the governess must choose between denouncing an abusive teacher, or accepting his behaviour (as his victims do) and living with the consequences of an ethical misjudgement. In *Pray for the Wanderer* Nell must choose between being respectable and unfulfilled, or choosing a life with Tom. In a discussion of the Basque missionary Francis

Xavier, O'Brien praised the Jesuit adherence to the "cold principle of abnegation" (quoted in Walshe, 2006b: 118), but throughout her work individual needs are the prime and necessary mover. Yolanda González Molano has suggested that O'Brien's focus on "the individual plane of the character's conscience, particularly in the case of female characters, results ... in a displacement of political issues [such as class or nation] onto the private sphere", and as a consequence, those issues become "muted" (2004: 145, my translation). But it can be counter-argued that O'Brien, like Helen Archer in *The Land of Spices*, "made a lifelong, personal study of the impersonal. Like a scientist perhaps, or a scholar" (2000b: 268), without a given agenda.

'Doing the right thing', no matter what its *denouement*, rarely brings about satisfaction to O'Brien's characters. In the words of Lorna Reynolds:

> The world of Kate O'Brien's novels is a sombre place, in the sense that men and women are shown as very rarely happy and when they are, but briefly. Her heroines, however, are the proof that she does not see happiness as the end of life. The end of life for women as for men is effort, achievement, the realisation of potentialities: it is love, not sexual satisfaction, and love is a gift that only freedom allows one to bestow. (1987: 129)

In another way, the very fact that her characters sometimes face unsolvable ethical problems indicates they are aware of new possibilities and powers in their pursuit of freedom.

PART II: POLITICS

Section One: nationalist

Kate O'Brien often claimed a lack of interest in politics, as we have seen in Chapter One, for example claiming in 1963 in *Presentation*

Parlour that "I was never much interested in political deviations and always concerned as to persons and their private decisions" (1994: 34). A number of critics—seemingly understanding 'politics' in the narrowest possible terms as party politics—have accepted this, arguing with Frank McNally that "politics—other than the sexual kind—was never ... her main theme" (2010: 15). In parallel, from the 1980s onwards, with the feminist reassessment of her work, and the fresh interest from a nascent institutionalised Irish Studies community besotted with her 'Irish Catholic dissent' agenda, a new orthodoxy of O'Brien the political icon was born. Feminist, queer, anti-colonial, and anti-de Valera readings of her work are now commonplace, as illustrated for example in the special issue of *Irish University Review* dedicated to O'Brien in 2018, or doctoral research such as Yolanda González Molano's on O'Brien and "Nation, Class, and Gender" (2004). A tendency to describe her work "as radical or subversive" has prompted Michael Cronin to remind us of "her commitment to bourgeois liberalism" (2010: 32). Liberalism is, nevertheless, a politics. The main ideological framework in political discussions of O'Brien to date is nationalism, but her relationship to it is more complex than it may at first appear.

From the point of view of politics, Kate O'Brien's work is always *located* in a particular socio-political space, most often in her contemporary Ireland. While internationalist ideology is rarely discussed in her books, her Europeanist commitment pushes her world towards the continent. Second only to Ireland, Spain is an important country in the O'Brienesque map of the world, followed by Italy, Belgium, and France. O'Brien is on the trail of Catholic Europe, and keen to let her sinful characters jostle with the prevalent status quo. Two politicians play important roles, the Basque communist Juanito Areavaga and the proto-fascist King of Spain Philip II, but O'Brien is more interested in power dynamics in small groups: nuns in Ireland, Irish governesses abroad, or a cosmopolitan artistic community in Rome. In terms of locatedness, her work has an Irish, ostensibly anti-nationalist, Europeanist character.

Irish

It is in O'Brien's Irish novels that the most explicit treatment of politics is found. A number of novels, such as *Without My Cloak*, *Pray for the Wanderer*, and *The Last of Summer*, are 'state of the nation' projects seeking to offer a fictionalised portrait of various sectors of Irish society at a specific moment in time. Her main focus is invariably the Irish Catholic middle class, a class which, it is often argued, she was the first to write about in fiction. Yet writers such as Rosa Mulholland and M.E. Francis, as James H. Murphy has discussed, used fiction to consolidate a developing Catholic Irish upper-middle class destined to become a post-colonial ruling class, sacrificing their own identity as women in the process—and Yolanda González Molano has contended that O'Brien follows the same model (see Molano, 2004: 145). The importance of the Irish content is as obvious as the particularly cosmopolitan tenor of that content. Karin Zettl has claimed that "Kate O'Brien located herself in a border zone between her native Ireland and the outside world and that border position shaped her narrative perspective" (2006: 41). She focused on 'the Irish abroad' in most of her post-1936 novels. When Angèle Maury arrives in Ireland at the beginning of *The Last of Summer*, on the eve of the Second World War, she will test Irish attitudes to the continent in general, and to fascist Europe in particular. Similarly, when Mary arrives in the Basque Country at the beginning of *Mary Lavelle*, on the eve of the fascist coup of General Primo de Rivera, and right after the creation of the Irish Free State, she will test the new possibilities opened to her own nation-state.

nationalist

An anti-nationalist position is articulated by several characters in

O'Brien's work. In *The Land of Spices*, for example, upon being told by a nationalist that Sinn Féin means 'ourselves alone', an English suffragette quietly states: "It's an unattractive motto to give to young people" (211). Yet it can be argued that this is not an anti-nationalist stance. Many Irish characters seek to create, at any cost, an Ireland that suits their needs. Matt Costello and Mary Lavelle have both had some involvement with the IRA. Half-Irish characters, from the Australian-Irish protagonist of *A Broken Song*, to the Spanish-Irish progeny in *Constancy*, seek ways of having their idiosyncrasies affirmed. Ireland is personified as a mother in several novels, from the tyrannical Hannah Kernahan in *The Last of Summer* and the irrelevant Teresa Mulqueen in *The Ante-Room*, to the cold and ineffectual Julia Delahunt in *The Flower of May*. But enterprising daughters such as Fanny Morrow or Jo Kernahan, or sons such as Denis Considine, are intent on creating or adopting alternative spaces, *owning* a different Ireland. In *The Flower of May*, Sharon Tighe-Mooney has contended, the personification of conservative Ireland, Julia, "must be literally killed off" (2014: 284). Thus, O'Brien's work can be seen as furthering a critical, progressive Irish nationalism; a self-aware allegiance to an Ireland-to-be, defined by connectivity and inclusiveness.

Europeanist

To O'Brien, Europe is the world. Partly as a reaction to Ireland's isolationist policy during the de Valera period, she was intent on yoking the country to the continent. O'Brien's work was, as an Irish bishop declares of a French school in *The Land of Spices*, "too European for present-day Irish requirements. Its detachment of spirit ... stand[s] in the way of nationalism" (2000b: 210). In the essay "Irish Writers and Europe" she described the eight centuries after Saint Patrick's death, when "[Irish] scholars and priests and poets were a peculiarly marked phenomenon of European life", as "our golden time" (1981b: 36). As we have seen,

O'Brien's Europe is emphatically Christian. The novels do not as much as mention Europe's colonial past, other than in terms of England's control of Ireland, and Christianity is presented as a civilising force, rather than, for example, as ideological channel or legitimator of imperialism. Possibly as a deformation of this entrenched Europeanism, O'Brien's work also presents an Islamophobic strain. It is explicit in *Farewell Spain* and implicit in *Mary Lavelle* and *That Lady*, often cloaked under a dislike of the Moorish-influenced Andalucian region in Spain. This racist aspect is unexpected in a body of work known, as we have seen, for its plea for mutual respect.

Section Two: socialist

Kate O'Brien's work has a notable strand of socialism, as well as a distinctly defined interest in anti-capitalism. It is important to acknowledge the difference in emphasis between them, however interrelated they may be. A shocked revulsion from the frenzy of productivity, product-consumption, and particularly the *display* of wealth, in New York, Bilbao, and Milan, is found in books as diverse as *Without my Cloak*, *Mary Lavelle*, and *My Ireland*. Anarchism, communism, socialism, federalism, and Marxist pragmatism, are all presented in a positive light in *Mary Lavelle*, *Teresa of Avila*, and *Farewell Spain*. Crucially, the span of O'Brien's publications intersected with the 'politicised 1930s' in Europe, often leaning left, but her references to Christian anarchism are inherited from the nineteenth century, specifically Tolstoy. The work of O'Brien may be said to be imbued with the sense of a radical Christianity—at odds with the Catholic church as a morality-obsessed institution—which is, first of all, *communitarian*. Consider this exchange between Father Malachi and Tom in *Pray for the Wanderer*:

> "I am not a militant Communist. I am a Franciscan."
> "In other words an anachronism". (1951: 121)

This notion is endorsed by Jesus himself, who appears as a secondary character in O'Brien's historical screenplay *Mary Magdalen*. Jesus is both a spiritual and a political leader, although "no foolish idealist", we are told, because his mission is "just plain materialism" (NLI, MS 19,703: 45). The same statement is made in the novel *Mary Lavelle* by the lawyer Juanito, a utilitarian advocate of state-communism, who has a strong anarchist vent and is a devout Catholic (see 2000a: 260). In the late nineteenth century, Christian anarchism found a compelling voice in the novelist Leo Tolstoy, who called for an end to the "immoral" class system—for example in an essay of 1897 titled "A Reply to Criticisms", which specifically seeks an end to colonial oppression in Ireland—and demands the dismantling of those "force-maintained anti-Christian combinations called states" (178).

socialist-realism

O'Brien's career coincided with widespread debates on the political role of art. As we have seen, one of the most influential strands of the debate was 'socialist realism', an aesthetic doctrine which demanded of politically committed writers that they combine "a truthfulness and historical concreteness" with the "remoulding and education of the toiling people in the spirit of socialism" (Zhdanov 1977: 21). Part of a wider purge of experimental art and literature, which had gone out of favour with Stalin's regime, the movement specifically opposed modernist writing. Writers around the world took note, and even those who counter-demanded aesthetic freedom, queried their own role as agents or *saboteurs* of change. Speaking to a group of international writers in Leningrad in 1963, O'Brien declared that: "The novelist's responsibility is immense—since his intention is to be read—by millions! But it is his sole responsibility, his inward duty, what he writes", and however "dangerous" it may seem to trust a writer to mediate between art and reality, the writer "has to do it alone" (O'Brien Papers, UL, doc 153: 1).

anti-capitalist

Throughout O'Brien's work, the display of riches is presented as more objectionable than wealth, and an emphasis on the "untidy" and "shabby" (*Mary Lavelle*, 2000a: 175, 71), often associated with sympathetic characters or truthful appearances, is presented by her as a counterweight model to a society obsessed with appearances. Consumerism and excess are a social pathology, as we see in the 'Denis in New York' section of *Without My Cloak* and in Mary Lavelle's exploration of Altorno/Bilbao. A nostalgia for the pastoral, together with the certitude of its disappearance, can be discerned in the shift from the Christina-Denis romance on the banks of the Shannon in *Without My Cloak*, to the distinctly un-Edenic Mary-Juanito sex scene in "The Good Basque Country" in *Mary Lavelle* (2000a: 302).

While the communitarian is normally set in contrast to individualism, and these terms are respectively aligned to socialism and market capitalism, in O'Brien's work everything is filtered through the individual, who has only the vaguest longing for connection to a group, a longing which generally goes unfulfilled. O'Brien hailed medieval Irish monasticism as "utopia[n]" (*My Ireland* 1962a: 25), but her nuns and monks fail to coalesce in the group; hence the only meaningful contact in the life of the protagonist nun in *The Land of Spices* is a thin thread to a child outside her own community. There are loose, small, diverse communities of friends and acquaintances in *The Last of Summer*, *Pray for the Wanderer*, and *As Music and Splendour*, which provide support and intellectual stimulus. In *Mary Lavelle*, Don Pablo and Milagros' individualist anarchism offers an outlook, and a set of rules for living, but Juanito is a politician: his centralised state-communism is designed as a pragmatic step in a Marxist-anarchist reading of history that predicts the dissolution of the state.

anti-authoritarian

An anti-authoritarian strand plays an important role in O'Brien's work, offering two dimensions: an interest in power structures in relationships and groups, and a registering of the growth and consolidation of fascism in Europe at the time of writing. References to authoritarian leaders are discussed in passing in novels and non-fiction from 1936 onwards, matching the rise of fascism in Europe and beyond. In *Pray for the Wanderer* the then Irish president de Valera, who ushered in a gender-retrograde constitution, enhanced the power of the Catholic church, and facilitated stringent censorship laws, is explicitly lined up as a menace to democracy:

> 'Artists are dangerous fellows—'
> 'Plato thought so', said Tom.
> 'So does Hitler,' said Matt. 'So does Stalin. So does Dev, I'll be bound!'
> (1951: 122)

In *That Lady*, the confrontation between Ana and her judge and jailer King Philip may be seen as a disquisition on the fascist mind, which is presented side by side with the articulation of "all that is individualistic, free and libertarian" (1985b: 150). As we know, *That Lady* was conceived in 1940, and Reynolds has suggested that Philip reflects "Nazi despotism and brutality", while the defiant Ana "may be seen as a prototype of the political martyrs of those war years" (1987: 73). Anthony Roche discerns a "complete fictionalisation of de Valera as King Philip II" (2018: 114), and Terry Eagleton suggests that the "absolutism" may be seen as "a displaced version of Roman Catholicism" (2009: 98).

Anarchism is positively presented in *Mary Lavelle* and its non-fiction companion book, *Farewell Spain*, with anti-authoritarian beliefs focused on 'the means, rather than the end'. In *Mary Lavelle*, a young Basque girl educates her Irish governess, in a deliberate reversal, on anarchist ideas. Besides timely, specific references to anarchism, O'Brien's work is interested in dissecting power, with the community leader in *The Land of Spices* as an example of a 'just ruler' keeping in check a motley crew headed by the authoritarian Mother Mary Andrew, and the matriarch in *The Last of Summer* as an example of a tyrant with a benevolent veneer, whose power is met by various forms of surrender or retreat to secure survival.

Section Three: queer (heterosexual & gay)

If O'Brien's work is concerned with "the relationship of sexuality to politics" (Meaney 1997: 81), it is particularly associated with the exploration of deviant sexualities and affects. Behaviours and identities that are seen as morally objectionable, outside the morally accepted norm, in the span of O'Brien's career, included extramarital relationships, female sexual assertiveness, and homosexual desires, the three rule-breaking behaviours most readily associated with her novels and plays. In terms of the representation of queer sexuality as a political threat to the status quo, there are a number of areas which mark O'Brien's work as remarkable: Ireland and sexual politics; sexual freedom, equality, or rights; representations of polyamory; gay rights; and queer politics.

Ireland: sexual politics

Sexuality is sometimes a symbol of politics in O'Brien. Individual young women embody Ireland's potential, caught unawares on the cusp of independence, stunned at an unexpected range of possibilities before her. The resolutions she makes in relation to her sexuality will determine her selfhood/nationhood henceforth: Fanny chooses sexual autonomy and comes to be represented by the lighthouse, the symbol of a new Ireland in *The Flower of May* (see Mentxaka 2018: 136), Angèle's conjugal skirmish confirms her embodiment of an exiled European-Ireland in *The Last of Summer*, while Agnes defers her own sexual needs for the sake of familial/national stability in *The Ante-Room*. The most obvious example of this allegorical strategy is, as we have seen, Mary Lavelle, twenty-two years of age in 1922, a governess who arrives in the Basque Country yearning for "self-government" (2000a: 27), a statement which unambiguously links the de-colonisation process to personal—pointedly, *sexual*—independence. Mary is "a green sort of creature" (2000a: 198), her innocence an oblique comment on the institutionalised Irish censorship which wants to keep her ignorant, but she has "grown up very fast" abroad (ibid: 307), and dares to express her sexual desires, exercising her freedom in a democratic gesture. Mary embarks on a romance with the communist Juanito, in a literary thought experiment: would a communist Ireland be viable?

sexual rights

Sexual freedoms, sexual equality, and sexual rights are crucial themes in O'Brien. Stories about relationships condemned by social mores, religious morality, or internalised censorship regularly present characters pressed into defying convention or abiding by it. As Sharon Tighe-Mooney has pointed out, "O'Brien took the unusual step, for her unmarried heroines, in portraying sexuality as a moral conflict within the context of romantic love" (2008: 126). Sexuality is the great meddler and shaper in all her novels. Lives are destroyed by sexual rebellion (*That Lady*), by moral revulsion (*The Land of Spices*), by the interference of relatives (*Without My Cloak*). O'Brien is particularly interested in couples with a status or wealth differential, and in women determined to make sexual choices. Her novels specialised in the challenges posed *to women* by extra-marital relationships, in some ways the supreme test of social rules within the merchant class, bourgeois world she focused on.

polyamory and celibacy

In O'Brien, illicit lovers engage in monogamous partnerships where true love is matched to promised or realised erotic fulfilment, but, as we have seen, remarkably for the period, polyamory is also presented as a viable option in some storylines. In *As Music and Splendour*, Luisa Carriaga has two lovers, one of whom has a preference for monogamy but accepts the arrangement in what has been described as a "utopian" gesture (Inckle 2006: 56). In the film script *Mary Magdalen*, the first century 'flapper' protagonist defends her right to sexual adventurousness, while in *Pray for the Wanderer*, Matt is happy to share Louise Lafleur with her husband Adam, but she decides she "can't belong physically to two people" because of her Huguenot scruples (1951: 90). In another unexpected move, intelligent and articulate characters in O'Brien often choose and defend celibacy as a life-option, on the libertarian basis that marriage may be simply too "exacting" because of "its ramified implications, the sheer measurelessness of its spiritual, emotional, and physical claims" (ibid: 163). In political terms, polygamy and celibacy appear to be harmless to the status quo, simply a matter of preference or conscience, but in fact they challenge normative marriage, one of its building blocks.

gay rights

We have discussed the representation of non-normative characters in Chapter Two, but a political impetus is a separate issue intersecting with representation. Gay rights are important, in that protagonists act as surrogates of prejudiced readers, when they are faced with homosexuality and are forced to decide how to respond to it, with some largesse. Gay characters such as Henry, Anna, or Clare are likable, but others like Luisa or Agatha seem calculated to keep a distance from the reader. In the 1930s, in *Pray for the Wanderer*, an Irish *maudit* points out that the "passwords" are "tolerance and discretion"; that is, "Go as you please and make no scenes" (1951: 73). Within those parameters, O'Brien's determination to include homosexual characters or references in every one of her novels has a political dimension.

queer politics

What would a queer politics look like in a literature subject to censorship such as O'Brien's? She criticised Henry James in 1963, in her essay "The Art of Writing", for his lack of (homo)sexual honesty: "He could be devious. He hinted overmuch; indeed, he could hint superbly, and to unerring purpose—but to hint is finally an artistic mistake, and can amount in art, as it can in life—to vulgarity" (1963a: 10). James "managed always to keep his gloves on" (ibid), O'Brien says, yet she was guarded herself. We have seen in Chapter One that in 1951 her biography of Teresa of Avila proposed that she had been lesbian. It is important to note here that, far from the 'politics of outing' developed in the 1980s (brash and confrontational public outings of contemporary closeted media figures), O'Brien had to rely on circumvention to make her point: Teresa's own account of engaging in "[that] pestilential pastime" (quoted in *Teresa of Avila*, 1993: 41) is given, and met with O'Brien's call for "caution", with the proviso that "Teresa's most learned and careful biographers ... are agreed in reluctance to measure her meaning" (ibid: 23). This convoluted statement is illustrative. A politics of explicitness was not fully available to either James or O'Brien, but a politics of inclusion was.

Section Four: feminist

According to Lorna Reynolds: "The subject of feminism is never openly raised in Kate O'Brien's work, but the theme of her novels is the necessity for woman to be as free as man", and novels such as *The Land of Spices* may be said to be "subtly but profoundly feminist" (1987: 128, 67). References to feminism, though rare, do feature, as in the biography of Teresa of Avila, where the counter-reformation religious leader is described as "a feminist" (1993: 111). A number of characters are informed by feminist ideas, from male courtiers to detached spinsters, and most storylines trace a woman's realisation and exercising of her own powers. This section considers the representation of feminism in her work, from three angles: characters and storylines which reflect individualist feminism; content which appears to reflect an anti-essentialist framework; examples of solidarity in a feminist context found in the work.

individualist feminism

Kate O'Brien's work registers an individualist feminism which is anti-authoritarian in nature. The only reference to organised collective feminist agitation in her fiction is a powerful one, and is again translated to an O'Brienesque idiom of personal choice. Miss Robertson in *The Land of Spices*, a suffragette holidaying in Ireland, has known prison and has likely gone on hunger strike, she declares, because of "an accident of time and place" (2000b: 210). Anna, a fifteen-year-old who has befriended her, feels that within her it "began to stir an uneasy understanding that liberty—she hardly knew for what, but just liberty, the general principle—might be an expensive thing" (ibid: 197). In the novels and plays, individual girls and women feel that their personal lives are circumscribed, but there is no explicit articulation of structural, systemic oppression. For example, in *Pray for the Wanderer* Una's serial child-bearing is questioned by a feminist male friend (Matt) as a self-negating practice, and spiritedly defended by her, as if it was simply a matter of individual choice, rather than a gendered convention with political implications (see 1951: 138–39).

against essentialism

O'Brien's work seems to run counter to gender essentialism—the notion that the sexes are naturally associated with given genders—by presenting fully human and flawed characters. Groups of women behave like villainous swarms in *Mary Lavelle* and *The Land of Spices*, and individual women in positions of power available to them, such as head of the family (Hannah in *The Last of Summer*), or teacher (Mary Andrew in *The Land of Spices*), often use their status to curtail other women's development. As we saw in the discussion on gender and sexuality, O'Brien tends to deliberately confuse gender categories. There is a type of woman that recurs in her stories: detached, intellectually rigorous, unemotional, and self-assured. It may well be that this is a strategy designed to undo contemporary views of 'the weaker sex' as convivial, intuitive, and prone to sentimentality. Consider the professional dreams of Anna Murphy in *The Land of Spices*:

> ...she desired to be a leader of brave fishermen, the strongest and best, when she read in the papers of the Balkan War just ending, she saw herself as a brainier Venizelos, and when she thought about Captain Scott she dreamt of the tragic and splendid expeditions she would lead, over even more desolate and heart-breaking Antarcticas. She thought of herself sometimes as a very heroic doctor, sometimes as a conductor of symphony orchestras, and sometimes as a humble and handsome Canadian 'Mountie'. (2000b: 207)

And her list goes on. It is 1913, and little Anna's list reads like speculative fiction, because these are all explicitly male vocations at that time.

solidarity

There is also solidarity between women. Agnes Mulqueen will not betray her sister in *The Ante-Room*, Agatha and Mary in *Mary Lavelle* will support their common friend's unconventional marriage, in *The Flower of May* Lucille will stand by her soul-mate even if the world wants them apart. In O'Brien, solidarity cuts across generations—aunt Eleanor Delahunt leaves the Glasalla farm to her niece instead of her nephews in *The Flower of May*, and Mary Lavelle's aunt leaves her in her will the hundred pounds which secure her independence, while Helen is instrumental in obtaining a scholarship for her young protegée in *The Land of Spices*. Women are also disablers of other women, from Mother Mary Andrew, to Julia Delahunt, to Hannah Kernahan (in *The*

Land of Spices, *The Flower of May*, and *The Last of Summer*)—sometimes for compelling reasons. Anna Teekell has contended, for example, that, "contrary to [traditional] readings" of *The Last of Summer*, "Angèle wishes to be disempowered, decided for. Hannah's feminine performance of neutrality [in the matter of her son's engagement to Angèle] is actually the more empowering" (2018: 108). Most tellingly, feminist men are outspoken in several novels. Antonio, a sixteenth-century courtier in *That Lady*, educates his lover proudly on all the "significant women in the world", listing "Margaret of Navarre, Elizabeth of England, Mother Teresa, the Princess of Eboli" (187); the absence of the finishing 'and' is a statement in itself. Matt Costello in *Pray for the Wanderer* and Eddy in *Without my Cloak* are more enlightened as to the patriarchal impositions on their female friends than the women themselves. The thirteen-year-old boy Charlie proudly wears a suffragette ribbon in *The Land of Spices*.

PART III: ACTIVISM

actively seeking change

Kate O'Brien's work did not just register political issues or ideas; it sought change, and it actively contributed to bring it about. As Eibhear Walshe put it, "[i]n her fiction, Kate O'Brien was a subversive" (2006b: 2). For all of O'Brien's genuine defence of the independence of creative artists, she used her fiction and non-fiction to further several causes. O'Brien was "proud" of the influence of Maria Edgeworth on Turgenev's *Huntsman's Sketches*, which contributed to the end of serfdom in Russia (O'Brien Papers, UL, doc 165: 308). An affinity with pacifism, anarchism, and feminism, a *sui generis* Irish nationalism with a European vocation, solidarity and support for the Spanish left in the fascist uprising and the dictatorship years, a determination to expand the scope of and a commitment to positive representations of homosexuality, are some of the more salient political strands in the work of O'Brien. In this section, we review the activist agendas in O'Brien's work: *to witness and document* issues in need of a platform; *to resist* conservative interventions; *to critique* normative ideology; *to protest* against attacks on artistic freedom; *to support* democracy under threat; and *to lead*, dismantling beliefs that underpin inequality, and reimagining and expanding ideological tools for change.

to witness and document

To witness and document, are two important functions served by O'Brien's work. We find that stories document abusive relationships, for example, presenting in print, with the finality of that gesture, various examples of child sexual abuse in the home, in teaching settings, and by strangers, from almost casual molestation (Angèle's uncle in *The Last of Summer*; Don Jorge's victims in his music class in *Mary Lavelle*), to grooming (Mr Lawson's tactic at Doon Point beach, in *The Land of Spices*), to sexual assault (Josie's attacker in "Manna"). What other Anglophone mainstream writer of her time made such a consistent effort to expose paedophilia? In a context of censorship, secrecy, and institutionalised abuse in Catholic Ireland, where sexuality itself was treated as objectionable, this is quite remarkable.

O'Brien's work also focused on queer lives, from heterosexual couples breaking barriers of class or ethnicity, to homosexual men and women determined to be themselves—stories make visible the plight of highly moral characters who feel that the natural rules of their hearts and desires clash with social expectations in life-crushing ways. O'Brien's insistence on bringing gay lives into her stories, with full rounded characters which see the world in their own terms, are particularly consonant with the present times, given the inordinately high value of literature as repository of gay knowledges, a documentation supressed elsewhere. The constraints placed upon women are to the forefront of the novels—again making it impossible to ignore the double-standards that make development or fulfilment almost unattainable for women.

In the context of the politics of her time, as an Irish writer's output, O'Brien's insistence on recording and making available debates which were foreclosed in public life in Ireland is a form of activism. She engaged with the normative anti-European bid for *cultural* self-sufficiency in de Valera's period of influence. The aim was not just to witness and document dissent, but to make injustice itself visible, as in the following conversation between the novelist Matt and his Irish friend Una in *Pray for the Wanderer*:

> 'I have a happy life—' [Una said]
> 'I know.'
> 'And I cannot see why millions of others—'
> 'Millions of others are slaving, Una, or workless, or homeless, or fighting in some brutal army for brutal ideologies they don't even begin to understand, or wasting in prisons because they resisted such ideologies, or hacking coal out of death-trap mines, or working overtime on incendiary bombs, or ranting away in manic-depressive wards because they should never have been born—'
> 'But these things needn't be. No decent person wishes it to be so—'
> 'Don't they? Anyhow, so things are.'
> (1951: 134)

Things As They Are was the title of an important activist novel of 1794 by the anarchist William Godwin, and like it, much of O'Brien's work aims at showing what others are determined not to see. "[I]gnorance is a passive form of denial", she explained in *My Ireland*, adding: "Ignorance denies the principles of beauty in all human majorities—nothing unusual in this—but the curious point about aesthetics is that in service of them minorities have tended, against odds, to win" (1962a: 99).

to resist

To resist, is one of the key motivations behind much of O'Brien's work. Eibhear Walshe suggests that "[h]er wartime writing was a kind of resistance writing, a response to censorship, to war and to her unstable working life" (2006b: 92). Her feminist and queer interventions also read as a form of resistance to conservatism. Despite her vocation to be outspoken, not everything could be discussed openly. One of the ways in which silencing could be circumvented was by using covert methods of communication. O'Brien specialised in literary connotation—in terms of aesthetics, as we have seen, she was interested in intertextuality and in building a web of references to enrich a text, but in political terms, she also knew she could print extraordinarily daring material if she presented it in the right guise. Mary Lavelle's tentative waywardness seems to have horrified the censors, but using a double male persona in *Pray for the Wanderer*, O'Brien was able to publicise outrageous sexual mischief with the freedom granted men, and she was even able to directly address the authoritarianism of the Irish state, and its censorship laws, without prompting a ban.

Almost unwittingly O'Brien became the flag of resistance in Ireland in 1946, as we have seen, with her open challenge to the Irish Censorship of Publications Act after the banning of her novel *The Land of Spices*. In fact, the campaign was orchestrated by Senator John Keane, who believed a successful challenge to the state could be mounted in the case of *The Land of Spices*, which appeared to have been banned because of a single sentence referring to homosexuality. As Eibhear Walshe has explained, the campaign "made Kate O'Brien something of an emblematic figure for liberal dissenters in Ireland", as well as "with Irish lesbians and gay men" (2006b: 44).

Through O'Brien's position as representative of Ireland at the European Association of Writers, the Communitá Europea degli Scrittori (COMES) based in Italy, she was directly engaged with debates among writers, including political discussions. The left-wing politicisation of writers in the 1930s and 1940s peaked at the Soviet Writers Congress of 1934 in Leningrad (carried out under the shadow of Stalinist control of the arts), where leading speakers demanded that all politically progressive writers throughout the world should adopt the tenets of socialist realism. Interestingly, the only text of O'Brien's participation at COMES debates kept among her papers is her address to the association at a meeting in Leningrad in August 1963, where, characteristically, she broke a lance in defence of *non-interference* by external forces in the creative process. In this context, it can be argued that throughout her career O'Brien also *resisted* directive intervention from the left.

to critique

To critique, is another motivator in O'Brien. We see it in the approach to Irish state policies during de Valera's 'reign', for example in the critique of Irish neutrality in World War II presented in *The Last of Summer*. The detached Irish Jo looks at the attractive French visitor Angèle, standing by her three brothers, and claims that "[f] or two pins I could make an analogy between you and Europe" (82). O'Brien desperately wants her readers to understand that she is presenting them with a 'thought experiment', to help them think through some pressing issues at the beginning of the Second World War, as Jo explains to Angèle:

> "You'll be all right here?"
> "Oh yes, Eire will be neutral, which is only the clearest common sense, politically. But that's beside the point. Little patches of immunity like ours are going to be small consolations for what's coming. Being neutral will be precious little help to the imagination, I should think." (1989: 81)

O'Brien's work also offers, as part of a disquisition on power-relations, a strong critique of the operations of the Catholic church, in its alliance with the Irish Free State, as we see in the discussions between Mother Superior and the local priest, or between the suffragette Miss Robertson and the Irish bishop in *The Land of Spices*, or as we see in the machinations of a priest who can wield his status to cover misdeeds and threaten obstructors, in the case of Don Jorge, in *Mary Lavelle*.

A critique of gendered norms is also important, including an ongoing study of the will-to-power in individual women who seek control over others, challenging the notion of women as repositories or parasitic dependents. In *The Flower of May*, for example, we are told that Lilian "is mistress of her beauty", which "she will invest … for sound dividends all her life" (1953: 206). Similarly, there is an activist's zealousness in wrestling romantic love away from stilted, normativised, and casually misogynist conventions as we see in *The Ante-Room*'s tension between Vincent's selfishness and Agnes's self-awareness.

Industrial capitalist comforts and middle-class complacency are sometimes presented as the photographic film positive, or obverse, of the degradation that makes them possible. This happens in the double-bind of Mary looking at the slums of Altorno from the lofty balcony of Allera Church, in *Mary Lavelle*, and Kate O'Brien looking back at her from those very slums, standing next to a rackety chapel and a young prostitute, "dilapidated" both, in *Farewell Spain* (204). As a traveller in the 1920s and 30s, O'Brien found Bilbao "very shocking" and Milán "disgusting" (quoted in Reynolds *Kate* 1987: 37; see O'Brien, 1962a: 19), but in her fiction she kept those unforgettable sights at bay. Instead, she mounted a critique of consumerism by developing frugality as the salient form of material engagement in all her heroines and heroes.

to protest

To protest, is another indicator of activism in the work of O'Brien. She protested against religious bigotry, the corralling of women, state censorship. As we know, in Ireland *Mary Lavelle* and *The Land of Spices* were both banned. In an article from 1934, published in England in *The Spectator*, O'Brien had already warned that president de Valera was "leading Ireland away from progress into isolation" (quoted by Zettl, 2006: 43), and two years later her own work would become a victim of 'Dev's' "dangerous moral philosophy, the new Calvinism of the Roman Catholic" in Ireland (1951: 30), as O'Brien's alter-ego Matt spells out in *Pray for the Wanderer*. The 1929 Censorship of Publications Act, nominally targeted 'indecent' or 'immoral' representations of sexuality, but its reviewing committee was not required to publicly explain its decisions. In 1936, as we have seen, *Mary Lavelle* was provocative for the conservative establishment on a number of counts. The new Ireland imagined in this novel, giving herself the freedom to make difficult choices, was not to be.

A year after the banning of *Mary Lavelle* in Ireland, Kate O'Brien published *Pray for the Wanderer*, whose protagonist is a banned Irish novelist self-exiled in England, who is outspoken about his predicament, acerbic about de Valera's authoritarianism, and concerned about the alliance of a retrograde nationalism and a misogynistic and sex-phobic Catholic hierarchy. Michael O'Toole described *Pray for the Wanderer* as her "novel of protest" (1995: n.p.), and James Cahalan called it "a literary revenge" (1988: 208). The book describes Ireland as "a dictator's country", declaring that president de Valera is "a more subtle dictator than most—though he also, given time, might have the minds of his people in chains" (1951: 30). We have discussed the significance of the Irish Constitution of 1937, and Sharon Tighe-Mooney has argued that the fact that "the conventional path of love and marriage does not transpire for O'Brien's single heroines ... in itself is a protest against a society that situated the family as the most important unit" (2008: 126).

Permission to publish *Mary Lavelle* was also denied by the Spanish censor, while references to Nazism in *The Last of Summer* had to be excised (see Ladrón, 2010). *That Lady* can be seen as a form of protest. Set in Spain under King Philip II, Eibhear Walshe has argued that it came out of O'Brien's "experiences of wartime censorship", with the protagonist as "an emblematic ... resistant woman", so when Ana "assert[s] ownership of her private life" O'Brien "extends this into a plea for democracy in Spain, subtly linking sexual and political authoritarianism" (2006b: 103, 105). As we know, it appears that O'Brien was forbidden entry into Spain until 1957, which upset her greatly, but in a 1977 talk she still described censorship of her work under Francoism as "the feather in my cap" (O'Brien Papers, UL, doc 166: 12).

to support

To support, is another central concern of O'Brien's activist work. In fiction and non-fiction, she put her weight on the side of the left in Spain, after the fascist uprising that was to result in a civil war followed by forty years of dictatorship by General Franco. The Spanish Civil War in fact elicited the most outspoken political statements in O'Brien's career. *Mary Lavelle* registered some of the social unrest which preceded the conflict, with the novel set in 1922 just before the coup of General Primo de Rivera—a timeline which allowed O'Brien to incorporate an apocalyptic subtext, an anti-capitalist parable suggesting that the amoral process of a sudden savage industrialisation, deserved to be punished by a cataclysm of biblical proportions (see Mentxaka, 2011: 151–55). Unknown to her at the time, such a fate was about to befall the Basque Country and Spain for a second time after her novel went to print, with a fascist military rising, followed by civil war.

O'Brien's *Farewell Spain* was one of the fastest literary responses to the conflict from Anglophone writers, and the most substantial Irish support for the democratically elected centre-left Spanish government. In the guise of a travelogue, *Farewell Spain* was designed, as we have seen, to rally support for the embattled republican government, by appealing to a broad readership, including those who primarily thought of Spain as a holiday destination ('Goodbye Tourism' was the title of the opening paragraph). Declaring its pacifist credentials, O'Brien makes a case for armed support of democracy, seeking to activate European states into assisting Spain. Positive accounts of communism and anarchism had been found in *Mary Lavelle*, and the travelogue furthers that avenue—explicitly distancing the Spanish left from Stalinism.

Farewell Spain lays out O'Brien's vision for a fascism-free Spain: an anarchist socialist organisational structure, federalist in principle—in this case honouring the cultural diversity within Spain and the historic rights of various regions (see 1985b: 224). This last issue had been raised in a more ambiguous fashion in *Mary Lavelle*, when in a gathering in the Basque Country, following a Madrilian's declaration of support for a non-partitioned and free Ireland, the Irish protagonist answers back with a challenge: "Do you then sympathise with the nationalist ambitions of the Catalans and the Basques?" (2000a: 152). While the novel appears to caricature Basque nationalism in the character of Juliana, Mary's own hunger for "perpetual self-government" is, as we have seen, an exercise in empathy (Ibid: 27; see 217). If there is support in *Mary Lavelle*, it is ambivalent or at least muted, perhaps in line with the "non-doctrinaire" O'Brien manifesto (1951: 119). *Farewell Spain*, written as an urgent appeal, spells out the support.

to lead

To lead, is part of O'Brien's activist agenda. Her work does not merely adopt or endorse ideas or projects, or support besieged or forgotten causes, but it also develops new thinking around resistance to capitalism, ethics of sexuality, the critique of gender, and anti-authoritarian ideas. In terms of anti-capitalist thinking, for example, O'Brien's develops a new aesthetic marker which is also a category of knowledge: 'shabby'. Placing the shabby between the beautiful and the Burkean sublime, she politicises aesthetics by striking an anti-capitalist match that makes neglect visible. Applied to places, such as the "shabbily baroque" *Place des Ormes* in Belgium or the Altorno square notable for "some shabby trees [and] a shabby bandstand" in *The Land of Spices* and *Mary Lavelle* (2000b: 152; 2000a: 71), the shabby can indicate authenticity, the neglect caused by poverty, or both. Applied to characters, such as a "shabby" gay sculptor from New York in *Without my Cloak*, or a "shabby" Basque anarchist historian with "irregular" features in *Mary Lavelle* (1986: 387; 2000a: 51), it is more than a bohemian trait, indicating substance, or contempt for the culture of display associated with market capitalism.

In a subsidiary strategy, O'Brien dissects and disables the concept of Beauty throughout her career, from *Gloria Gish* onwards—for example, the most relevant thing about Mary Lavelle's extraordinary beauty is her own contempt for it, and the most relevant thing about Lilian Morrow's beauty in *The Flower of May* is that "[s]he wears it like a weapon" (1953: 206). In the Western imaginary, beauty is a quality of intrinsic value, and it is associated with idealised femininity. O'Brien's approach here is therefore part of her pioneering critique of gender. As a thinker, she also leads in her treatment of sexuality. For example, O'Brien's novels give expression, as we have seen, to a non-proprietorial ethics of sexual partnerships (through Clare Halvey, Matt Costello, Ana de Mendoza, or Catherine Archer) which is rather out of step with the conservatism of the 1930s, 40s, and 50s, and her novels also defend celibacy as a legitimate option, whether in or out of religious contexts.

O'Brien also made inroads with her contribution to feminist and lesbian historiography in *Teresa of Avila*, and her promotion and elucidation of anarchist ideas in *Farewell Spain* and *Mary Lavelle*. Some of her allegories made anti-authoritarian ideas intersect with feminism and post-colonial experience in interesting ways. For example, O'Brien suggests an equivalence between a woman's realisation of her potential and the post-colonial process, when aunt Eleanor gives Fanny "a weapon of independence" by gifting her the family farm in *The Flower of May* (1953: 251). For example, after little Charlie Murphy's accidental drowning in *The Land of Spices*, in a place associated with a paedophile's predatory activities, Charlie's body is found with his beloved women's suffrage ribbon on his chest, suggesting that the sexual abuse of children and the subjection of women stem from the very same structural oppression. For example, all O'Brien novels provide studies of power structures from various angles, often placing misogyny in a continuum of authoritarianism (attuned to Woolf's formulation in *Three Guineas*), as in Philip's imperialist "absolutism" in state and personal matters, which impoverishes "our national life, our home life", in *That Lady* (1985a: 107).

Kate O'Brien's work also leads in that it gives shape to a different kind of nationalism. If we define nationalism as an 'allegiance', rooted in the belief in the cultural distinctiveness of a community, and energised by the desire to further that community's development, then O'Brien's work is an expression or articulation of a form of Irish nationalism. The Ireland imagined in her novels has an outward shape mirroring its inward components. For example, Heather Ingman has noted that the nuns' convent school of *La Compagnie de la Sainte Famille* [tr. The Companions of the Holy Family], "provides a site of resistance to Irish nationalism", and it "functions as an alternative to the family unit enshrined as the basis of de Valera's Constitution, an alternative which, for Anna at least, is more positive and nurturing than Anna's real family" (2006: 207). Ingman reads this intervention as "irony" (ibid), but it can equally be said that this convent, this novel, are a thought experiment in trying to imagine an Ireland that can absorb multiple interests and beliefs, built on Christian compassion and communitarian values, bringing Irish culture and a European vocation together.

AFTERWORD

> James Joyce and Kate O'Brien are an incongruous pair—
> the former the giant of male Irish writers, the latter one of
> the least recognised of Irish women writers. Yet people once
> laughed at the idea of comparing Shakespeare with Jane
> Austen. They don't any longer. (Donovan 1988:19)

This was printed in 1988, in a fiery pamphlet on the marginalisation of Irish women writers, by Katie Donovan. It becomes increasingly obvious with time that there are many Irish Austens the world needs to rediscover. Some still-marginalised work may supplement our understanding of O'Brien, such as the blazing modernist Christian-atheist poetry in *Firehead*, by Lola Ridge (1924), or the thriller-documentary fiction on the Basque resistance and the Spanish Civil War by Shevawn Lynam *The Spirit and the Clay* (1954). Current trends of O'Brien criticism continue the discussion of gender and sexuality, begin to assess her modernist credentials, and investigate lesser studied material such as her plays. Margaret O'Neill's forthcoming monograph *Kate O'Brien's Writings* (2022) throws light on the socio-cultural impact of her work. A collection of O'Brien's criticism, in preparation by Jana Fishcherova, will no doubt lead to fresh inquiries into her role as public commentator. The study of O'Brien can lead in many other directions, including back to the nineteenth-century New Women writers (as Tina O'Toole has highlighted). Still, comparative analysis between O'Brien and forebears such as

George Egerton or Emily Lawless is yet to emerge. And on a wider radius, how about links to melodramatic, sensation novels of the kind written by Hall Caine, which made such an impression on the young Kate? How about placing her work in relation to *conceptual* novels, written on two (or more) simultaneous cognitive levels, such as some of the novels of Elizabeth Bowen? How about tracing O'Brien's anti-authoritarian family tree backwards, forwards, sidewise, to the fiction of William Godwin, Ursula le Guin, Ethel Voynich? How about studying O'Brien as a Spanish-Irish writer, and the last writer of the 'Generación del 98'?—I suspect she would be pleased by that.

I opened this book remembering the community of O'Brien scholars. So many more than those mentioned have formed the connective tissue of this book, and so many more are still emerging, that I am only too aware of this silent army marching towards unknown fields in O'Brien Studies. Many scholars who began their careers in earnest, with O'Brien's work as their flying standard, have since fallen on the side of the road to a professional career, exhausted by an academic ethos of precarisation, and the commodification of culture. It is to them that I would like to dedicate this book, and remind of the co-ownership of all our scholarly efforts.

BIBLIOGRAPHY

O'BRIEN, KATE

novels
---. (1951). *Pray for the Wanderer* (1938). London: Penguin.
---. (1953). *The Flower of May*. London: Heinemann.
---. (1985a). *That Lady*. (1946). London, Virago.
---. (1986). *Without My Cloak* (1931). London: Virago.
---. (1989). *The Last of Summer* (1943). London: Virago.
---. (2000a). *Mary Lavelle* (1936). London: Virago.
---. (2000b). *The Land of Spices* (1941). London: Virago.
---. (2005). *As Music and Splendour* (1958). Dublin: Penguin.
---. (2006). *The Ante-Room* (1934). London: Virago.

non-fiction
---. (1943). *English Diaries and Journals*. London: William Collins.
---. (1962a). *My Ireland*. London: B.T. Batsford.
---. (1985b). *Farewell Spain* (1937). London: Virago.
---. (1993). *Teresa of Avila* (1951). Cork and Dublin: Mercier Press.
---. (2001). *Presentation Parlour* (1963). London: House of Stratus.

plays
---. (1926). *Distinguished Villa: A Play in Three Acts*. London: Ernest Benn.

short stories
---. (1935). 'Overheard', short story. *Time and Tide*, 2 March 1935.
---. (1942). "Singapore has Fallen". *The Spectator*, 21 February 1942. Kate O'Brien Papers, University of Limerick (UL). Doc 141.
---. (1956). "Boney Fidey" (w. 1956). Kate O'Brien Papers, University of Limerick (UL). Doc 144.
---. (1962c). "Manna" (w. 1962). Kate O'Brien Papers, University of Limerick (UL). Doc 145.

essays and articles

---. (1938). "Why the Rage for French Films?" *The Star*, 1 February 1938, n.p. Kate O'Brien Papers, University of Limerick (UL). Doc 134, 12.
---. (1955). "As to University Life", *University Review*, Vol 1, No. 6 (1955): 3–5.
---. (1957). "Limerick, as I remember it". *Limerick Feile Padraig 10–17 March 1957* programme. Limerick: Limerick City Council, p. 50.
---. (1958). "Lennox Robinson". *University Review*. Vol. 2, No. 5 (1958): 58–9.
---. (1962b). "UCD as I forget it". *University Review*. Vol. 3, No. 2 (1962): 6–11.
---. (1963a). "The Art of Writing". *University Review*. Vol. 3, No. 4 (1963): 6–14.
---. (1981a). "'Long Distance' column: The Irish Times Extracts". [1962–1972]. Selected by John Liddy. *Stony Thursday Book*. John Jordan guest ed. Issue 7 (1981): 34–35.
---. (1981b). "Irish Writers and Europe" [1965]. *The Stony Thursday Book*. John Jordan guest ed. Issue 7 (1981): 36–7.

archival material

---. (w.c.1930?) *Gloria Gish: A Comedy in Three Acts*. Undated and unpublished typescript. National Library of Ireland (NLI). MS 36,179.
---. (w.c.1930?) *Mary Magdalen*. Undated filmscript. National Library of Ireland (NLI) MS 19,703.
---. (w.c. 1934?). *A Broken Song*. Undated filmscript. Kate O'Brien Papers, University of Limerick (UL). Doc 185.
---. (1963b) [Leningrad Address: 'The Writer Must be Left Alone']. Untitled and unpublished address. COMES international conference. Leningrad, August 1963. Kate O'Brien Papers, University of Limerick (UL). Doc. 153.
---. (1966) "Ireland and *Avant-Gardisme*". Unpublished lecture. May 1966. Kate O'Brien Papers, University of Limerick (UL). Doc 157.
---. (1971) "Imaginative Prose of the Irish"/ "La Prosa Imaginativa of ficcional en Irlanda a partir de 1800". Lecture, December 1971, University of Valladolid. Kate O'Brien Papers, University of Limerick (UL). 165.
----. (1972a) *Constancy*. Kate O'Brien Papers, University of Limerick (UL). Doc 175.
----. (1972b) ["Spain"]. Untitled and unpublished lecture, delivered to the Association of Professional and Businesswomen, Canterbury, 10 March 1972. Kate O'Brien Papers, University of Limerick (UL). Doc 166.

Secondary Sources

Abel, Elisabeth, Marianne Hirsh, and Elisabeth Langland (1983). "Introduction". *The Voyage In: Fictions of Female Development*. Elisabeth Abel et al eds. Hanover (NH): University Press of New England, 3–21.
Areilza, Enrique. (1999). "Gredos" [1917]. *Epistolario*. JM Areilza ed, Bilbao: El Tilo, 225–26.

BIBLIOGRAPHY

Areilza, Jose María. (1997) "Mary Lavelle", in *Tres Batallas por Bilbao y otras Páginas*. Bilbao: El Tilo, pp. 226–29.

---. (1994). "Kate O'Brien: A Personal and Literary Portrait" (1989). *With Warmest Love: Lectures for Kate O'Brien 1984–93*. John Logan ed. Limerick: Mellick Press, 33–41.

Augustine. (1966). *The Confessions of St Augustine* (w.c. 400), Trans. E.B. Pusey. London: Everyman.

Battersby, Eileen. (1997). "What Kate wrote: dissecting the bourgeois mind". *The Irish Times* online. 20 Feb 1997. www.irishtimes.com/culture/what-kate-wrote-dissecting-the-bourgeois-mind-1.44773. accessed 1 Sept 2020.

de Beauvoir, Simone. (2011). *The Second Sex* [1949]. Translated by Constance Borde and Sheila Malovany-Chevallier London: Vintage.

Bell, Clive. (1914). *Art*. London: Chatto & Windus.

Bergson, Henri. (1971). *"Time and Free Will: An Essay on the Immediate Data of Consciousness* (1889). London: Allen and Unwin.

Boylan, Clare. (2000). "Introduction", Kate O'Brien, *The Land of Spices*. London: Virago, vii-xii.

Boland, Eavan. (1994). "The Legacy of Kate O'Brien" [1985]. *With Warmest Love: Lectures for Kate O'Brien, 1984–93*. John Logan ed. Limerick: Mellick Press, 1–14.

---. (1981). "Introduction", Kate O'Brien, *The Last of Summer*. London: Virago, v-xv.

Bowen, Elizabeth. (1980). "Unwelcome Idea", of 1941]. *Collected Stories*. London: Vintage, 573—577.

Brady, Deirdre. (2015). "An Irish Literary Set that was more Bloomsbury than Barstool". *The Irish Times* online. 7 May 2015. www.irishtimes.com/culture/books/an-irish-literary-set-that-was-more-bloomsbury-than-barstool-1.2203909 Accessed 1 sept 2020.

Breen, Michelle. (2017). "A treasure trove of letters from Limerick author Kate O'Brien". 10 March 2017. *UL Library News & Events*. www.ul.ie/library/about/news-events/treasure-trove-letters-limerick-author-kate-o%E2%80%99brien Accessed 1 Sept 2020.

Brief Encounter (Dir. David Lean, 1945).

Burke, Edmund. (1990). *A Philosophical Enquiry into the Rising of our Ideas of the Sublime and Beautiful* (1757). Oxford: Oxford University Press.

Butler, Judith. (1993). "Critically Queer". *Bodies that Matter: On the Discursive Limits of 'Sex'*. New York and London: Routledge, 223–242.

Cahalan, James. (1988). *The Irish Novel*. Boston: Twayne.

Callaghan, Louise C. (2003). "Kate O'Brien". Unpublished paper. *An Evening with Kate O'Brien* conference, University College Dublin, 16 January 2003.

Clear, Caitríona. (2009). "Kate O'Brien, convents and class" [1998]. *Faithful Companions,* Mary Coll ed, Limerick: Mellick Press, 50–9.

Coughlan, Patricia. (1993). "Kate O'Brien: Feminine Beauty, Feminist Writing and Sexual Role". *Ordinary People Dancing: Essays on Kate O'Brien*. Eibhear Walshe ed. Cork: Cork University Press, 59–85.

Cronin, Michael. (2010). "Kate O'Brien and the Erotics of Liberal Catholic Dissent". *Field Day Review.* Vol. 6 (2010): 28–51.

Cullingford, Elizabeth Butler. (2007). "'Our Nuns are not a Nation': Politicising the Convent in Irish Literature and Film". *Irish Postmodernisms and Popular Culture.* Wanda Balzano et al eds. London: Palgrave, 55–73.

Dalsimer, Adele. (1990). *Kate O'Brien, A Critical Study.* Dublin: Gill and Macmillan.

Davison, Jane. (2017). *Kate O'Brien and Spanish Literary Culture.* Syracuse (NY): Syracuse University Press.

Donoghue, Emma. (1993). "'Out of Order': Kate O'Brien's Lesbian Fictions". *Ordinary People Dancing: Essays on Kate O'Brien.* Eibhear Walshe ed. Cork: Cork University Press, 36–59.

---. (2009). "Embraces of Love" (1996), *Faithful Companions,* Mary Coll ed, Limerick: Mellick Press, 2009, 16–31.

Donovan, Katie. (1988). *Irish Women Writers—Marginalised by Whom?* Letters From the New Ireland series. Dublin: Raven Arts Press.

Eagleton, Terry. (2009). "Love and Art in Kate O'Brien" [2001], *Faithful Companions,* Mary Coll ed, Limerick: Mellick Press, 92–99.

Faderman, Lillian. (1985). *Surpassing the Love of Men: Romantic Friendship and Love between Women from the Renaissance to the Present* [1981]. London: Women's Press.

---. (1995). *Chloe Plus Olivia: An Anthology of Lesbian Literature from the Seventeenth Century to the Present* [1994]. Harmondsworth: Penguin.

Fischerova, Jana. (2018). "The Banning and Unbanning of Kate O'Brien's *The Land of Spices*". *Irish University Review.* Paige Reynolds guest ed. Vol. 48, No. 1 (Spring/Summer 2018): 69–83.

---. (2019). "Kate O'Brien as Critic and Public Intellectual". Unpublished paper. IASIL Conference, Trinity College Dublin, 24 July 2019.

Fogarty, Anne. (1993). "Desire in the Novels of Kate O'Brien". *Ordinary People Dancing: Essays on Kate O'Brien.* Eibhear Walshe ed. Cork: Cork University Press, 101–120.

---. (2014). "Women and Modernism". Joe Cleary ed. *The Cambridge Companion to Irish Modernism.* Cambridge and New York: Cambridge University Press,147–160.

Foster, R.F. (2015). *Vivid Faces: The Revolutionary Generation in Ireland 1890–1923* (2014). London: Penguin.

Goldman, Alan H. (1977). "Plain Sex". *Philosophy and Public Affairs.* Issue 6 Number 3 (Spring 1977): 267–287.

Leeney, Cathy. (2004). "Ireland's 'Exiled' Women Playwrights: Teresa Deevy and Marina Carr". *The Cambridge Companion to Twentieth-Century Irish Drama,* ed. Shaun Richards. Cambridge: Cambridge University Press, 150–161.

Hayes, Elizabeth M. (1978). "Kate O'Brien: An Approach". Unpublished MA thesis. University College Dublin.

Heaney, James. (2009). "Time and Place in *The Land of Spices*" [1999], *Faithful Companions,* Mary Coll ed, Limerick: Mellick Press, 60–74.

Hemingway, Ernest. (1960). *Death in the Afternoon* [1932]. New York: Scribner's.

Hogan, Desmond. (1985). "Introduction". Kate O'Brien, *That Lady*. London: Virago, v-xiv.
Howie, Peter C. (2012). "Philosophy of Life: J. L. Moreno's Revolutionary Philosophical Underpinnings of Psychodrama and Group Psychotherapy". *Group*. Vol. 36, No. 2 (Summer): 135–146.
Inckle, Kay. (2006). "Tragic Heroines, Stinking Lilies, and Fallen Women: Love and Desire in Kate O'Brien's *As Music and Splendour*". *Irish Feminist Review*, Issue 2 (2006): 56–73.
Ingman, Heather. (2007). *Twentieth Century Fiction*. Aldershot: Ashgate.
Jordan, John. (2006a). "Kate O'Brien: First Lady of Irish Letters" [1973]. *Crystal Clear: The Selected Prose of John Jordan*. Hugh McFadden ed, Dublin: Lilliput Press, 227–230.
----. (2006b). "Kate O'Brien" [1976]. *Crystal Clear: The Selected Prose of John Jordan*. Hugh McFadden ed. Dublin: Lilliput Press, 233–235.
---. (2006c). "Kate O'Brien" [1987]. *Crystal Clear: The Selected Prose of John Jordan*. Hugh McFadden ed, Dublin: Lilliput Press, 236–239.
Kiberd, Declan. (2000). *Irish Classics*. London: Granta.
Ladrón, Marisol Morales. (2010). "Banned in Spain? Truths, Lies, and censorship in Kate O'Brien's Novels". *ATLANTIS, Journal of the Spanish Association of Anglo-American Studies*. Vol. 32, No. 1 (June 2010): 51–72.
Laverty, Maura. (1986). *No More than Human* [1944]. London: Virago.
Lawrence, Margaret. (1937). *We Write as Women* [1936]. London: Michael Joseph.
Ledger, Sally. (1997). *The New Woman: Fiction and Feminism at the Fin de Siècle*. Manchester: Manchester University Press.
Lee, J.J. (1979). "Women and the Church since the Famine". *Women in Irish Society: The Historical Dimension*. Margaret McCurtain and Donncha Ó Corrain eds. Westport, CT: Greenwood Press, 37–45.
----. (1989). *Ireland 1912–1985: Politics and Society*. Cambridge: Cambridge University Press, 1989.
Levinas, Emmanuel. (1981). *Otherwise Than Being; or, Beyond Essence* ([1974]. London: Martunus Nijhoff.
Lewis, Thomas S.W. (1983). "The Brothers of Ganymede" [1982]. *Salmagundi*. Issue 58/59 (Fall 1982–Winter 1983): 147–165.
Logan, John. (1994). "Family and Fortune in Kate O'Brien's Limerick". *With Warmest Love: Lectures for Kate O'Brien, 1984–93*. John Logan ed. Limerick: Mellick Press, 105–130.
McAuliffe, Mary. (2000). *Margaret Skinnider*. Dublin: University College Dublin Press.
Meaney, Gerardine. (1997). "Territory and Transgression: History, Nationality, and Sexuality in Kate O'Brien's Fiction". *Irish Journal of Feminist Studies*. Vol. 2 Issue 2 (Dec 1997): 77–92.
---. (2010). "Introduction". *Gender, Ireland, and Cultural Change: Race, Sex, and Nation*. New York: Routledge, xi-xx.

Mentxaka, Aintzane L. (2011). *Kate O'Brien and the Fiction of Identity*. Jefferson (NC): McFarland.

---. (2016). *The Postcolonial Traveler: Kate O'Brien and the Basques/ La Viajera Poscolonial: Kate O'Brien y Euskadi*. Palo Alto (Ca): Academica Press.

---. "Kate O'Brien and Virginia Woolf: Common Ground" (2018). *Irish University Review*. Paige Reynolds guest ed. Vol. 48, No. 1 (Spring/Summer): 127–142.

Milton, John. (1900). *Paradise Lost: Books I & II* [1667]. J. Sargenaunt ed. London and New York: Edward Arnold.

Mittermaier, Ute Anna. (2017). *Images of Spain in Irish Literature, 1822–1975*. London: Peter Lang.

Molano, Yolanda González. (2004). "Molly Keane y Kate O'Brien: Nación, Clase, y Género", unpublished PhD thesis, Universitat Autónoma de Barcelona.

Montaigne, Michel de. (1993). "On Friendship" (1576). *Essays*. J. M. Cohen ed. and translator. Harmondsworth: Penguin, 91–105.

Montalbán, Josu. (2008). *El Doctor Areilza: Médico de los Mineros*. Bilbao: Muelle de Uribitarte.

Moran, James. (2018). "Kate O'Brien in the Theatre". *Irish University Review*. Paige Reynolds guest ed. Vol. 48, No. 1 (Spring/Summer 2018): 7–22.

Morris, Catherine. (2012). *Alice Milligan and the Irish Cultural Revival*. Dublin: Four Courts Press.

New Jerusalem Bible: Study Edition. (1994). Henry Wansbrough ed. London: Darton, Longman, and Todd.

O'Connor, Elizabeth Foley. (2014). "Kate O'Brien, James Joyce, and the 'Lonely Genius'". *Joycean Legacies*. Martha C. Carpentier ed. London: Palgrave, 11–32.

O'Mara, Stephen. (1921). "Memorandum from Stephen M O'Mara to Eamon de Valera" New York, 12 August 1921. *Documents on Irish Foreign Policy*. www.difp.ie/viewdoc.asp?DocID=106 accessed 1 Sept 2020.

O'Neill, Mary. (1985). "Introduction". Kate O'Brien, *Farewell Spain*. London: Virago, ix-xxi.

O'Toole, Fintan. (2001). "Introduction". Kate O'Brien. *Presentation Parlour*. London: House of Stratus, 1–6.

O'Toole, Michael. (1993). "The Art of Writing – Kate O'Brien's Journalism". *Ordinary People Dancing: Essays on Kate O'Brien*. Eibhear Walshe ed. Cork: Cork University Press, 128–136.

---. (1995). "Peasants to Princes". *Management – Journals of the IMI (Irish Management Institute)*, December 195, n.p.

O'Toole, Tina. (2000). "Kate O'Brien (1897–1974)". *Lesbian Histories and Cultures: An Encyclopaedia*. Bonnie Zimmerman ed. New York and London: Garland, 555.

---. (2013). *The Irish New Woman*. London: Palgrave.

Oliver, Miquel dels Sants. (1974). "La Literatura del Desastre" [1907]. *La Literatura del Desastre*. Barcelona: Ediciones Península, 69–122.

Proust, Marcel. (2003). *Sodome et Gomorrhe* [1921–22]. London: Penguin.

Reynolds, Lorna. (1987) *Kate O'Brien, A Literary Portrait*. Gerrards Cross. Buckinghamshire: Colin Smythe.

---. (1994). "Kate O'Brien, Artist and Feminist" [1990]. *With Warmest Love: Lectures for Kate O'Brien, 1984-93*. John Logan ed. Limerick: Mellick Press, 51-62.

Reynolds, Paige. "Spectacular Nostalgia: Modernist and Dramatic Form in Kate O'Brien's *Pray for the Wanderer*". *Irish University Review*. Paige Reynolds guest ed. Vol. 48, No. 1 (Spring/Summer 2018): 54-68.

Riviere, Joan. (1989). "Womanliness as Masquerade" [1929]. *Formations of Fantasy*. Victor Burgin et al eds. London: Routledge, 35-44.

Robb, Graham. (2003). *Strangers: Homosexual Love in the Nineteenth Century*. London: Picador.

Roche, Anthony. (1993). "*The Ante-Room* as Drama". *Ordinary People Dancing: Essays on Kate O'Brien*, Eibhear Walshe ed. Cork: Cork University Press, 85-101.

---. (2018). "'The Devil Era': The Presence of Éamon de Valera in Three Novels by Kate O'Brien". *Irish University Review*. Paige Reynolds guest ed. Vol. 48, No. 1 (Spring/Summer 2018): 113-126.

RTÉ Television. (1962). *Kate O'Brien: Self-Portrait*. Documentary. Broadcast 28 March.

Rubin, Gayle. (1975). "The Traffic in Women: Notes on the 'Politic Economy' of Sex". *Toward an Anthropology of Women*. Rayna Reiter ed. New York: Monthly Review Press, 157-210.

Santayana, George. (1955). *The Sense of Beauty, Being the Outline of Aesthetic Theory*. New York: Dover.

Sedgwick, Eve Kosofsky. (1990). *Epistemology of the Closet*. Berkeley and Los Angeles: University of California Press.

---. (1992). *Between Men: English Literature and Male Homosocial Desire* (1985). New York: Columbia University Press.

---. (1993). "Queer and Now". *Tendencies*. Durham: Duke University Press, 1-20.

Smith, James. (2004). "The Origins of Ireland's Containment Culture and the Carrigan Report", in *Journal of the History of Sexuality*. Issue 13, No. 2 (2004): 208-33.

Smith, Paul. (1994). "[Kate O'Brien:] A Personal Memoir" [1991]. *With Warmest Love: Essays for Kate O'Brien*. John Logan ed. Limerick: Mellick Press, 99-104.

Teekell, Anna. (2018). "No 'Help to the Imagination': Kate O'Brien and the Emergency". *Irish University Review*. Paige Reynolds guest ed. Vol. 48, No. 1 (Spring/Summer 2018): 97-112.

Tighe-Mooney, Sharon. (2008). "Sexuality and Religion in Kate O'Brien's Fiction". *Essays in Irish Literary Criticism: Gender, Sexuality, and Corporeality*. Deirdre Quinn and Sharon Tighe-Mooney eds. Lampeter: Edwin Mellen Press, 125-39.

---. (2014). "Towards a Critical Reappraisal of Kate O'Brien's *The Flower of May*', *Irish University Review*. Issue 44. No. 2 (2014): 272-87.

Tiernan, Sonja. (2012). *Eva Gore-Booth: An Image of Such Politics*. Manchester: Manchester University Press.

Tolstoy, Leo. (1968). "A Reply to Criticisms" [1897]. *Tolstoy's Writings on Civil Disobedience and Non-Violence*. London: Peter Owen.

Travis, Charles. (2009). "The 'Historical Poetics' of Kate O'Brien's Limerick: A Critical Literary Geography of Saorstát Éireann and the 1937 Bunreacht na hÉireann Plebiscite". *Irish Geography*. Vol 42, No. 3 (2009): 323–341.

Vega, Suzanne. (1991). "On Masculinity". *Squire*. October 1991.

Walshe, Eibhear. (2006a). "Invisible Irelands: Kate O'Brien's Lesbian and Gay Social Formations in London and Ireland in the Twentieth Century". *SQS journal*. Issue 1, No. 6 (2006): 39–48.

---. (2006b). *Kate O'Brien: A Writing Life*. Dublin and Portland (OR): Irish Academic Press.

---. (2018). "Kate O'Brien". *A History of Irish Women's Literature*. Heather Ingman and Clíona Ó Gallchoir eds. Cambridge: Cambridge University Press, 227–43.

---. ed. (1993). *Ordinary People Dancing: Essays on Kate O'Brien*. Cork: Cork University Press

Ward, Margaret. (1989). *Unmanageable Revolutionaries*. London: Pluto Press.

Warner, Michael. (1999). *The Trouble with Normal: Sex, Politics, and the Ethics of Queer Life*. New York: Free Press, 1999.

Weekes, Anne Owens. (1990). *Irish Women Writers: An Uncharted Tradition*. Kentucky: The University Press of Kentucky.

Wilde, Oscar. (2002). "De Profundis" [w. 1897]. *De Profundis, The Ballad of Reading Gaol, and Other Writings*. Ware: Wordsworth.

Woodcock, George. (1970). *Anarchism* [1962]. Harmondsworth: Penguin.

Zhdanov, Andrei. (1977). "Soviet Literature: The Richest in Ideas, the Most Advanced Literature" [1934]. *Soviet Writers' Congress 1934: The Debate on Socialist Realism and Modernism in the Soviet Union*. HG. Scott ed. London: Lawrence and Wishart, 15–26.

Zettl, Karin Eva. (1993). "'In Search of a Personal Position': Women's Quest for Individuality in Kate O'Brien's Novels *The Ante-Room* (1934), *Mary Lavelle* (1936), and *That Lady* (1946)". Unpublished MA Thesis, University College Dublin.

www.ingramcontent.com/pod-product-compliance
Lightning Source LLC
Chambersburg PA
CBHW052047300426
44117CB00012B/2015